Just a Year, Lord

Daily readings
from the writings of Flora Larsson
edited and arranged by
Major David Dalziel

With an introductory memoir by
Commissioner John Larsson

United Kingdom Territory of The Salvation Army
101 Newington Causeway, London SE1 6BN

MAJOR DAVID DALZIEL
is Literary Editor of The Salvation Army
United Kingdom Territory

Cover photgraph by Lieut-Colonel Miriam Frederiksen
Mts Tasman and Cook, New Zealand
Cover design by Gill Cox
Typeset by THQ Print and Design Unit
Produced by THQ Literary Unit

Printed by Page Bros (Norwich) Ltd

Preface

FLORA LARSSON'S work has been popular for many years. Her early writings were mostly contributions – both poems and prose – for Salvation Army periodicals, or short biographies of well-known Salvationist personalities, culminating in her major work *My Best Men are Women*.

But Flora is best known for her five books of prayer poems, the first of which, *Just a Moment, Lord*, was published by Hodder and Stoughton almost thirty years ago. Translated into many languages, the poems struck a chord with readers all over the world. In Norway alone, over 100,000 copies of these books have been sold.

This volume contains many of those prayer poems, now regrettably out of print, together with biographical and other thought-provoking snippets culled from various sources. Selections from *Along the Way* (a column for the women's magazine *The Deliverer*) can be found alongside articles written for the Finnish *War Cry* under the titles *Ur Minnets Gömmor (Down Memory Lane)* and *Levnadsråd (Hints for Living)*. The book also contains a little material previously published in *From My Treasure Chest*.

Readings are arranged with a thought, a poem or a short article for each day of the year including one for leap year, 29 February. Articles relating to the movable feasts of the Christian calendar, Easter and Whitsun, will not usually fall on the right day, though the dates chosen are the commonest on which those celebrations fall throughout the next four decades!

The international flavour of these writings reflects the life experience of their author. She served as a Salvation Army officer with her husband Sture, in Britain, Sweden, Denmark, Chile (with Bolivia and Peru), Argentina (with Uruguay and Paraguay), France (with Algeria), Finland and Norway (with Iceland and the Faeroes). They retired from International Headquarters, where Commissioner Sture Larsson was the International Secretary for Europe, in 1974. Later that same year the commissioner was promoted to Glory, leaving Flora to experience 25 years of retirement alone.

I wish to express special thanks to Lieut-Colonel Miriam Frederiksen, Flora's daughter, who has provided biographical background and the typescript (in English, fortunately) of many articles. Miriam also pointed out her own favourites from amongst her mother's writings, and took the photograph which has been used for the cover.

Thanks to all those involved in production of this volume, especially to Major Trevor Howes who read the manuscript and proofs and gave much technical advice, to Robert Fox who formatted the pages, and to Captain Charles King who suggested the title, *Just a Year, Lord*.

D. D.

A BIOGRAPHICAL MEMOIR

Flora Larsson – My Mother

Commissioner John Larsson, Chief of the Staff,
introduces his mother to her readers through words spoken at the
Thanksgiving Service for her life and ministry held on 20 March 2000

MY mother was a citizen of three countries. British by parentage, Swedish by marriage and Argentinean by birth, she had three passports. But she had a fourth passport as well! One of her favourite songs was number 176 in *The Song Book of The Salvation Army*, written by Olive Holbrook. Its last verse reads:

> *This is the lamp to pilgrim given,*
> *This is my passport into Heaven,*
> *Portent of immortality,*
> *That God, through Jesus, dwells in me.*

My mother's fourth passport was her Heavenly passport! 'This is my passport into Heaven – that God, through Jesus, dwells in me!'

Passport troubles

My mother had known passport troubles in her life. When in 1949 we as a family were headed for Chile, we travelled via Argentina. My mother was travelling on a Swedish passport. She had left Argentina, where her parents were pioneer officers, when only a baby. On arrival in Buenos Aires, a zealous immigration official spotted the fateful words in her passport – Place of birth: Buenos Aires.

Here was trouble. Why was she not travelling as an Argentine citizen? Why had she not voted in all elections since she was 21? Serious matter this!

She would have to take out an Argentine passport before she could travel further. The matter was eventually resolved by the compromise arrangement that my mother had to report to the police once a day for the week we stayed in Buenos Aires. Three years later in Chile my parents got word that their next appointment would be in Argentina. My mother knew she had to get the passport question sorted out. She went to the Argentine consulate and explained – and after much toing and froing finally got her Argentine passport.

On the departure day we went to the airport. Everyone was there to say goodbye. We sailed through immigration. We were headed for the plane on the tarmac when suddenly an official came running. 'That lady there! There's a problem. She came into the country as a Swedish citizen and is now leaving as an Argentine citizen!' Explanations were fruitless. Surely she should have known that the new passport had to be countersigned by this ministry and double-stamped by the other. Somebody should have told her. The situation had to be regularised.

In the end, my father, my sister Miriam and I had to fly on to Buenos Aires, leaving my mother behind. After scurrying from one ministry to the other to get the right stamps in her passport, she joined us the next day.

But a few days ago, as my mother began her greatest journey, her passport – the Heavenly passport – would have been in perfect order. Her first sight of the other side might well have been a reassuring sign reading: 'Heavenly passport holders – this way.' And her passport into Heaven was this: that God, through Jesus, dwelt in her.

'It is a strange thought,' she once wrote, 'that I shall embark on the last journey with no ticket, no luggage and no money, I who have always made such careful preparations for every little trip. This time there will be just me … and You, Lord.'

For her final journey – no ticket, no luggage, no money. But a passport – yes! All holders of a Heavenly passport reveal in their lives and personalities something of the qualities of a citizen of Heaven. When I think of my mother I think of:

The grace of a questing mind

My mother was intensely alive mentally. Exploring the universe was a continual quest for her. For her, life was an adventure. Life was meant to be lived positively and to the full – and with a sense of fun.

She loved the world of books. In her latter years the mobile library service couldn't keep up with her. Until within a few months of her death at the age of nearly 96 she was 'a book a day' person – re-reading her favourites many times. She followed new research avidly, through books and through TV, and when Miriam and I lived abroad her letters would often include cuttings or extracts from what she had been reading. From time to time she herself engaged in detailed research on a variety of topics – especially when she was preparing a new book.

When she was still able to get out on her own, it used to be a family saying that something always happened to her. She met someone, or saw something, or got caught up in some event, and as soon as she got home she would sit down and write it up for her page in the quarterly magazine *The Deliverer* – a page she wrote for 18 years.

She was ahead of her time in her thinking about the Army. At times she could be quite radical in her ideas. Sometimes around the kitchen table when Miriam and I had been discussing the Army with our parents, we teasingly used to comment that it was a good thing father was the territorial commander and not mother – for who knows where the Army might end up! She believed wholeheartedly that this questing and exploring would continue into the next life. For her it was part of being a Heavenly passport holder. Another characteristic of hers was:

The grace of empathy

In going through her papers we came to a bulky folder marked 'letters from readers'. It makes moving reading. But the content of that file is only a fragment of the influence she exercised through her writings, through her speaking – for she was a captivating speaker in any of the six languages she had mastered – or through her personal and telephone ministry to those in need of encouragement

She had the gift of empathy. She could enter into people's thoughts and feelings in such a way that people felt that they knew her, even when they had never met her. When she wrote about cooking for one, about an awful day, about spring and sun and laughter, they identified with her. She put into words what they themselves were feeling. Wherever we have travelled in the world someone has come up to say thank you for her writings.

The names Flora and Freda have a certain similarity, and over the years Freda – my wife – has developed into a fine art the skill of deflecting gracefully the comment: 'Mrs Larsson – your writings have meant *so* much to me.'

When we visited a certain corps in New Zealand a lady was very anxious to speak to me alone. When we retired into a corner, she told me how her life had gone to pieces when her husband died. What saved me, she said, was Flora Larsson's prayer poem 'Courage to live'. She then opened her purse, took out a wrinkled piece of paper that had been folded small, unfolded it and read to me the whole poem, which starts:

Lord, give me courage to live!
A cheerful courage, Master, if that might be.
Let me wear a smile even when my heart trembles ...

Said the lady to me: 'I have given away copy after copy of that poem to others – for it saved my life.'

Jesus knew what was in people – empathy is a characteristic of the citizens of Heaven. Another quality of Heaven seen in my mother was:

The grace of spiritual awareness

We often draw a contrast between the Marys and the Marthas of this world. To a remarkable degree, my mother seemed to have the qualities of both – she had the gift of spiritual sensitivity and the gift of being down to earth and practical. She had moments of intense spiritual experience – fleeting but unforgettable moments. She describes such a moment that came to her when watching a sunset:

I saw Heaven open, Lord...
I looked right through the clouds to the heart of being,
the limpid glowing heart of being,
shining through wisps of brightness.
The sense of distance was immense and breath-catching.
In the breaks of the serried clouds lay pale green islands
fringed with red-gold haze,
In all that far-searching stretch of Glory
I felt I belonged, Lord.
I wasn't a tiny human pigmy dwarfed by natural splendour,
cowering down in fear;
I was a child of the universe, at home in the universe
because I knew You, its Creator.
In those few moments I lived,
enthralled, uplifted, enraptured,
while time stood still.
All my being was suffused with radiant joy.
I was at one with You, Lord of life.
Slowly, quite slowly, the sheer bright glory faded;
dusky shadows stole across the sky.
The sense of awareness dulled, receded,
but I had seen and felt and I can never forget.

Master, is this a foretaste of what you have in store for us
in the life to come?
If so, why should anyone be afraid?

In just such a moment of mystic experience she discovered God had given her the gift of spiritual healing. She had been praying about that gift for some time. Then in a time of spiritual breakthrough, in Finland, she felt a warmth in her hands – which she took to be God telling her that the gift was hers. She wrote in a *War Cry* article of her first faltering attempt to use that gift. She described how, when sitting on the platform in the Thursday united holiness meeting, she remembered that one of the cadets, seated in the body of the hall, was suffering from an incurable condition whereby her fingers were slowly bending inwards. It was thought that the cadet would have to return home.

When it came to the prayer meeting my mother had an intense conviction that she should do something. She would need a translator, for Finnish was not one of her languages, and she was shy of drawing attention to herself. But she went down, and invited the cadet into the officers' room. Never having done anything like this before she wasn't sure how to proceed. But she placed her hands just above the cadet's hands and began to pray.

Nothing happened. As she put it in her article, the little imp that lives in her mind said to her: 'See, what a fool you have made of yourself!' But she kept on praying. After what seemed like a very long time the cadet said: 'I can feel heat in my hands.' And it appeared that the fingers had slightly more movement. My mother and the cadet met a number of times for prayer – and each time the fingers loosened more and more. Finally the hand was completely healed. The cadet became an officer and gave a lifetime of service to the Lord.

Heavenly passport holders have that kind of intimacy with their Lord. His power flows through them. But Flora Larsson was also a Martha. She had:

The grace of practicality

My mother ran her household and garden with the precision of a ship's captain, and was amazingly inventive when it came to solving everyday practical problems. Her creativity was not confined to the fields of writing and speaking, and we would often be amused by her latest exploit. In Chile, after baking and icing a birthday cake, she left it in the oven – only to find it black with ants when she returned. The next day every leg of the kitchen appliances and furniture stood in a saucer of water. The ants never solved that one!

She was determined that when she went to the Lord everything left behind would be in impeccable order. She had worked out that no one in her family had lived beyond the age of 86, and she saw that as the likely date of her departure. In good time she started clearing out and giving things away – so we would have less to do when she went. She in fact established a new family record by living nearly 10 years beyond what she thought to be her allotted span. But in those intervening years it was hard to know what to give her for Christmas – for she didn't want anything that would add to the eventual clearing! She was so practical that I wouldn't put it past her to have arranged with the Lord for him to fetch her Home on a weekend when we happened to be home.

As a Heavenly passport holder, she had another beautiful grace:

The grace of simplicity

She wanted her writing to be direct and simple. Like her Lord and Master, she sought for the vivid word-picture that remains in the mind.

When as a boy I began exploring at the piano keyboard the mysterious riches of harmonic consonance and dissonance, she would often say: 'Keep it simple, John.' When as a teenager I might have dreamt of writing massive works for brass and voice using Schoenberg's 12 tone scale – works that would leave the hearer baffled and, hopefully, impressed – that voice kept coming to mind: 'Keep it simple, John.' Those four words were a strong influence on my music writing style.

She had a simple and practical faith too. She recounts in her writings of the time when she and my father were visiting a cathedral town in France and they lost the car keys. They retraced their steps – but to no avail. And then in typical fashion she said to the Lord: 'Lord, you know where the keys are! Please lead us to them.'

There was an immediate answer in the form of a strong conviction. 'Ask the policeman!' The only gendarme visible was the one standing in the middle of the busy intersection, directing the traffic. She made her way through the procession of cars, and asked him if he had seen the keys. While blowing his whistle and directing the traffic with the one hand, he opened the other, and said: 'Are these they, Madame?' They were!

Yes, there was a beautiful simplicity to her life, her writings, her faith. The final quality I want to mention is:

The grace of acceptance

My mother never complained about the limitations that advancing years put on to her. With the vivid choice of phrase that characterised her writings, she once said to me: 'John, old age is damnable.' But she said it with a twinkle in her eyes. And that revealed to me the grace of acceptance.

It almost became embarrassing to ask her: 'How are you today?' for her invariable reply was: 'I'm all right, thank you. I am always the same.' And she kept saying that to the end. I think she will have smiled and felt pleased that on her death certificate the doctor gave as cause of death nothing more than 'old age'. Quite an achievement!

She captured that grace of acceptance in a word picture that deserves to be quoted in full. It is entitled 'Dangling Leaves':

I saw them in the park this morning, Lord,
and I chuckled to myself, for I'm just like them.
Other leaves had withered and fallen,
obeying nature's mysterious laws,
but a few individualists remained dangling on the branches,
weathered pennants of a season's storms.
Withered, yes, their rich colours fading,
but still alive
and – if leaves can kick – kicking.

They were enjoying themselves dancing in the autumnal gusts
and my heart danced with them.
They exulted in the strong wind, even mocked it, I felt,
for still they hung on,
grimly but triumphantly.
My season is over too, Lord, but I hang on
with sufficient strength and humour to make it worth while.
The sap of life still flows in my veins,
enough to withstand life's tempests.
Though wrinkled and faded, I'm still game.

One day some harsh frost or boisterous wind
will get the better of me.
My tenuous hold on life will snap
and my body will return to the soil where it belongs,
yielding itself willingly to Mother Earth
while my spirit returns to You.
Until then, Master, keep my courage high.
Let me play the game right to the finish
then not quarrel when the end comes.
It's been a good life, Master, with Your aid.

The grace of acceptance!

The Heavenly passport

With her Heavenly passport in her hand Flora Larsson has arrived in her Homeland – where she truly belongs. She is at home, and as she herself wrote:

Don't let my loved ones sorrow for me when I go, Lord.
Let them think of me emerging into more abundant life
with much greater fulfilment
and added joys.
Let them remember that I shall still be in Your hands,
still the object of Your love and care,
and let their hearts be comforted.

And our hearts are!

BEGIN AGAIN (NEW YEAR)

HOW many times, Lord, must I make
    a new start?
How often must I confess to You
    that I have failed?
Failed in my Christian duty,
    in my relationships,
    in my prayer life
through inertia, busyness or apathy.

What a quagmire of undesirable traits
    mushed up together
    in an unsavoury bog
that clogs my footsteps on the Christian way!
You must be tired of listening
    to the dreary catalogue
    of my shortcomings
just as I am tired of confessing them.

And yet something within me urges:
    try once more!
    Begin again!
I believe, Lord, it is Your voice in my heart,
    Your Spirit within me
that lights a faint glimmer of hope
    in the depressing darkness.

Dare I make a new start? I hesitate . . .
    reflect . . .
glimpse the abyss of despair yawning at my feet.
I clench my will to action as I say:
    'I'll try, Lord!'
'I throw myself upon Your mercy and by Your grace
I'll begin again. So help me, God.'

                      God in My Everyday

YESTERDAY

YESTERDAY is an old garment, Lord,
   creased, stained and threadbare.
   Help me to throw it off,
   casting it into the coffers of the past,
   done with, laid aside and forgotten.

Let me not walk in my yesterdays;
   not live again the used-up hours,
   regretting the misspent moments,
   brooding over the rebuffs,
   fingering the tattered glory-rags,
   clutching them close to my eager breast.

Today is new, fresh from Your hands,
   glowing with promise of fulfilment,
   full of opportunities,
   of duties,
   of joys;
   with perhaps a tinge of sorrow.

Let me wear 'today' hopefully,
   grateful that it is mine,
   glad to face its challenge,
   using unstintingly
   each moment as it comes.

For tonight, Master, tonight I must lay it off,
   an old garment,
   creased, stained and threadbare,
   casting it into the coffers of the past,
   done with, laid aside and forgotten.

Just a Moment, Lord

MY FIRST MEMORY

MY earliest recollection dates back to the time when I was only three or four years old. I see a small girl – myself – hiding behind the heavy curtains in the front room.

From whom am I hiding? From my brothers and sister.

Why? Because I have something in my hand which is good to eat and I don't want to share it with them.

What can it be that I am so secretive about? A cream cake? A box of chocolate? No, nothing so expensive as that. Just four tiny sweets clutched in my hot little hand.

Someone had given me a farthing, the smallest English coin, and I had run quickly to the sweet shop to spend my wealth. Not daring to eat on the street in case anyone saw me, I hid behind the curtains and one after another pushed the sweets into my mouth and hastily swallowed them.

I can still remember the feelings which filled my heart. The sweets did not taste as nice as usual because I had to eat them so hastily, listening hard to hear if anyone was coming. And a very real feeling of shame made me feel unhappy. I had been selfish and greedy, keeping all four sweets to myself.

How strange that this early memory still lives with me 60 years later! Many more important things have been forgotten. Yet this first memory is etched on my mind as if I had a photograph of the scene. It reveals how sensitive the mind and heart of a child can be. I never confessed to anyone what I had done. I had not stolen the farthing, but had come by it by doing some small duty for a neighbour. So it was mine to do with as I liked. And yet my conscience upbraided me for selfishness.

I had thought that by going behind the curtains I could be in peace, but I learnt at a very young age that there is a voice within the soul of man that cannot be shut out. The voice of conscience.

Ur Minnets Gömmor (Down Memory Lane)

ALLERGIC TO YOURSELF

AT home I have a book where some years ago I pasted in a series of comic cartoons that I cut out of newspapers and magazines.

One is a picture of a man being examined by the doctor. The doctor says: 'This is a very serious allergy. You are allergic to yourself!'

If we don't like ourselves enough to be happy in our own company as often as is necessary, then something is wrong.

Hints for Living

FROST

MASTER, I don't like frost.
I don't like to feel it, that is.
It looks attractive enough in the garden
     silvering the grass, highlighting the twigs on the trees
     sparkling in the clear, cold moonlight,
     but in my bones I hate it.

It does ugly things to me,
     my hair goes stringy, my nose and eyes run,
     my joints complain
and *I* complain too, Lord.

Help me to weigh the good against the bad.
     Frost is purifying, stimulating.
It breaks up the garden clods
(and from the shelter of indoor warmth,
     I smugly survey the few yards I have dug)
and it cleanses the atmosphere.
Best of all, it doesn't last forever.

It's one of those things that come and go,
     so why make a song about it, or rather a moan?
Common sense tells me to accept it without complaint,
without feeling it is somehow personally directed against me.
There's the rub, Lord, not only for me but for many others
who regard what happens as a malevolent attack
     because it interferes with our desires.
Make me more flexible, Master, more able to accept what comes
without losing my mental equilibrium.

Between You and Me, Lord

MINE WERE REAL TEARS

WHEN my younger brother and I were too small to go to the Sunday night meeting, Mother used to hold a little service for us at home. One evening, she spoke tenderly about Jesus dying on the cross for the sins of the world and told us that even our childish sins were included in his great redemption. I presume she asked us if we would like to be 'saved', and we both assented.

    I was about six and my brother four years old. We knelt at Mother's knee and she prayed for each of us. What effect that prayer had on our childish souls I do not know. The immediate effect on me was, however, regrettable. Both my brother and I had been touched by Mother's gentle appeal and tender prayer and as we knelt the tears had fallen. Now we stood up, and as we wiped our eyes the dogma of original sin with pride as its first-fruit received its confirmation by my reaction.

I looked with childish contempt at my little brother's reddened eyes. 'Mine were real tears,' I said to myself, 'he is only crying because he saw me do it.' Poor Mother! She never knew how her just-saved little daughter reasoned within her own small mind.

I never reckon that moment as my conversion – and I'm sure it does not stand in the Heavenly register either. Mother's prayers and God's love for me conquered later on in my life. Perhaps many of us come to God in that way – little by little, step by step, yet finally all the way.

Ur Minnets Gömmor (Down Memory Lane)

REGRETS

MASTER, did You live with regrets?
At the close of the day when quick darkness stole over Palestine,
     and you looked back over the hours,
did You regret anything that had happened that day?
Not what other people had done or said,
but what You Yourself were responsible for?
     Did You, Lord? I wonder . . .

Were You so perfect that You always said the right word at the right
     time?
     That You always did the right act at the right moment?
     That your thoughts and reactions were immediately
     what they should be? I really wonder . . .

I remember You in Gethsemane,
     with the shadow of a harsh cross looming ahead;
with the horror of 'being made sin' – what loathsome degradation –
     darkening Your path:
You hesitated . . . You struggled with Yourself, but You conquered.

And that remembrance helps me,
     for I am not always what I want to be,
     I am not always what I ought to be,
     so each evening is tinged with regret.

In Your rich mercy will You grant me a favour?
Will You give me courage to begin again each morning, dear Lord,
     as if the day before had never been?

Between You and Me, Lord

MY FIRST BOOK

ONCE, on a visit to Norway, I was asked by a group of students at The Salvation Army's folk high school how and when I started to write.

That question certainly re-awoke old memories! It took me to an old house in Liverpool, to a copy book which I hid in a bedroom drawer and wrote in at every spare moment of my school days. It was quite naturally a school story, for that was all I knew of life at the age of 14. Chapter after chapter followed in my rather untidy writing.

For weeks I was absorbed in the task. Then came reaction. A shock wave of disbelief rolled over me as I re-read my manuscript. It was flat, insipid and uninteresting, even to my biased judgement. I dared not proceed with it. For weeks the manuscript lay untouched but safely hidden. I knew that most great authors fell to the depth of despair over their writings, particularly their first works. I knew, too, what they did with their manuscripts, the carefully covered pages bearing their inward thoughts.

I would do the same.

Down at the bottom of the garden I started a bonfire and laid my precious pages on it, watching as they curled, browned and blackened with the heat. I knew that all great authors cried when their manuscripts shrank to ashes in the flames so I, too, cried a few tears.

And that was the end of my first book.

Along the Way

A BLOW BELOW THE BELT

ON this same visit to Norway, I stayed at a hotel which offered a word for the day in a number of languages at the breakfast table. On attractive small cards, various mottoes and quotations were printed and one could choose one's language and take the card away. There was only one card in English and I felt that its message was like a blow below the belt.

It quoted from Proverbs 6:6, 'Take a lesson from the ants, you lazy fellow. Learn from their ways and be wise.' What a thought for the day for a hard-working woman doing her best!

Along the Way

LOVING YOURSELF (1)

SOME people mistake what Jesus said about loving God and our fellow man. Jesus did not tell people to love their neighbour better than themselves, but as much as themselves.

In a healthy life there must be self-respect, self-acceptance, a reasonable self-love.

We must like ourselves if we are going to like others.

Hints for Living

BOOK FRIENDS

I'M grateful, Lord,
    for the many friends on my bookshelf.
Some of them are in old and worn covers,
    clearly ripening into extreme age
    and liable to be regarded as lumber
    by the uninitiated
yet more precious, more cherished by me as time passes.

What a privilege to sit down, stretch out a hand
    and draw a friend to your side,
    an old and trusted friend
    to whom one loves to listen.
So well-known are these old books that I can open
    them anywhere
    and feel at home, relaxed,
    refreshed by long-loved words and stories.

Sometimes, Master, I think of the writers,
    most of them already in the Beyond,
how they gave of the rich upsurgings of their heart
    not knowing into whose mind their words would
    fall
yet linked in close friendship with their readers
    of many generations.

I want to thank You, Lord, for the riches that come to me
    through books and other writings,
    for the uplift of inspiring thoughts,
    the widening of my interests,
    the raising of my hopes.
Bless all those who write
    and those who produce the printed word.
Let their standards remain high so that future readers
    may tread the pleasant upland paths that I have
    trod,
and be helped in their ascent towards You.

Between You and Me, Lord

THE IMP

IN the back of my mind, Master,
resides the imp.
Who and what he is I don't know, but he
        makes caustic comments
        on all I say or do.
In a way I suppose he keeps me in order,
for his running remarks have acted
        as a brake or a spur on many occasions.

'You a Christian!' he scorns.
'You're a fine example, I must say.
Look at the chances you have let slip today
        of showing your colours
        or saying a word for your Lord!'
But the very next day he can mutter:
        'That was splendid! You really shone!
        People were very much impressed . . .'
and I realise that he is tempting me to be proud.

Sometimes I wonder if he is my conscience
        but I am sure he is more than that.
He is me, outside me, observing me
all the time
        and analysing my motives,
        criticising my actions
        and querying my decisions.
It is quite difficult to live with this imp
ever with me,
        but I know of no way to get rid of him.
Is he for You, or against You, Master?
        I am never quite sure.

My God and I

A BLIND INSIGHT

ONE day, I found myself standing beside a blind man at a bus stop. As the
wait was long, I got into conversation with him. Wondering what subject
might be useful to begin with, I remarked on the extremely noisy traffic
rolling by. 'Oh, I don't listen to it,' he answered cheerily. 'I fix my thoughts
on something nice – a pleasant country lane or a rose garden – and then the
traffic doesn't annoy me.

I congratulated him on being such a philosopher, but it came as a rebuke to me that this man without sight could teach the seeing a valuable lesson.

As our bus drew near I wondered how I could best help him, but he was equal to the occasion. As he heard the bus draw up, he stretched out his hand to feel it, guiding himself along to the steps. In the bus I sat beside him and we continued our conversation.

Such an optimistic, cheerful passenger I have seldom met. I regretted that my journey by his side had to be so short, and we parted good friends.

Along the Way

FRIENDSHIP

YOU, Master, knew the worth of friends
    and drew them close to You.
From Your seventy-two evangelists
You chose twelve disciples;
From those twelve an inner circle of three
and from that trio one special friend
    closer to Your heart and mind
    than any of the others.
The strength of it! To have a human face,
    a human voice and heart
reaching out in staunch support.

So You understand our need of friends
and our pleasure when we find them.
Help us to treasure the bond of friendship,
treating it as a precious privilege
    to be used but not abused.
Let us not be demanding of time,
    interest or involvement.
Preserve us from thinking that we own our friends,
or that they owe us something.
Let us not stretch the links between us
    to breaking point.

Thank You, Lord, for friends
    past and present.
Above all, for Your companionship.

God in My Everyday

APPROACH

SOMETIMES, Lord, You come unheralded,
You enter by the side door of my heart
and are there almost before I am aware of Your nearness.

It was so today,
there at home in the living room
as I sat with a book among children and grandchildren.
Suddenly You were there beside me,
  I knew it, I felt it,
  for my heart warmed and quickened
  to Your presence,
  and a flush of joy filled me.

What unlatched the door of my heart to You, Master?
  Was it the book I was reading
  or the nearness of loved ones?
Often when I pray I don't feel You near,
but when I was not praying, You came.

Teach me the secret, Master,
of preparing a way of entrance for You
so that I can oftener feel You near,
  feel that sudden uplift of the heart,
  that stirring of the thoughts
  which heralds Your approach.

I wish I knew how to keep the door open,
  forever open to Your welcome intrusion.
Perhaps I am asking too much?
But thank You, Lord, that at times my blundering
   efforts succeed
in swinging open the door to allow You to pass.
May it happen more often, is my prayer.

Between You and Me, Lord

WHO MAKES CHAIRS?

WHO makes chairs? Men or women? Until now most have been designed by men and I sometimes wonder whether they get anyone to try them.

In the Army hall where I worship, a broad piece of wood cuts right into my shoulders, just where I am trying to sprout angel's wings. After a meeting my shoulders feel sore and at times I try to imagine the shape of the person who tried out the chairs for comfort.

Or is the idea to keep us awake by means of minor discomfort?

In a train recently I had to sit with my neck forward and my back hunched to fit the cushions. I decided that either a dwarf or a giant had tried out the models and approved them for public transport.

Or is it I who am wrongly made? I wonder . . .

Along the Way

A LIVING CONTACT

LORD, I want to be a living contact for You,
     a link between You and other people.
I've known You for so many years now,
     that I can recommend You to others who need You.

People do need You, Master, but they don't realise it.
They want to be happy and loved,
     to find a meaning to life.

They don't understand that only when lived with You
     can life find its truest expression.

They carry a hidden burden of conscience-distress
     and fail to see that only You can forgive sin
     and lift the load from them.

They complain of boredom and frustration, not knowing
     that You can add an extra dimension to their lives.
They are dissatisfied and unhappy, not realising
     that You can provide the missing ingredient.

So that is why, Lord, I want to be a living contact for You.
I want to tell people what You have done for me and others.
Sometimes I feel that I'd like to stand in the market-places
     of the world
     and shout aloud for all to hear;
     crying not my own wares, but Yours.

Help me, Master, in my own way and just where I am,
     to be a living contact for You,
     a link between You and other people.
     For they do need You.

Just a Moment, Lord

SIDETRACKS

THE picture did not tell the whole story, Lord.
    I remember it clearly
for it made a great impression on my childish mind,
the narrow gate leading through many adventures to life,
the broad gate leading straight to the fires of hell.
        It was a sermon in itself,
        harsh and vivid,
        frightening to a young mind.

To my mature mind it seems that the artist had got one
           thing wrong.
        He didn't show the sidetracks.

He depicted two distinct roads each governed by its entrance.
Experience has taught me that many are the sidetracks
        that lead from the narrow path to the broad:
        the way of compromise,
        the way of ease,
        the way of lowered ideals,
        neglect of the means of grace, and many others.

Lord, these sidetracks are not clearly marked.
        They open so easily, so pleasantly, so conveniently;
        they follow parallel for a time,
        and their final destination is hidden.

How am I to know which is the true narrow path,
        and which the false sidetrack,
        when they look so alike?

Master, I have passed through the narrow door at Your call,
and I am trying to keep on the right road.
At each fork will You help me to choose aright?
        For I want to follow the Way of Life,
        which leads to Your Heavenly mansions.
                        Just a Moment, Lord

THE UPWARD PULL

EACH year in the early months we see 'the upward pull of unrealised potentiality' as the bulbs thrust their vigorous shoots into the cold air and short daylight. It never fails to fascinate me and to preach to me a new sermon about the greatness of the Creator-God who sustains such a wealth of variety. In a moral sense we people also feel the upward pull of unrealised potentials. There is something which stretches us beyond the requirements of the everyday, which demands of us an obedience, a discipline, a striving after something higher and better than we have hitherto known.

I'm glad it is so; that as Christians we never reach the extent of our potentiality as spiritual beings; that there are always higher heights, wider horizons, new questings open to us and beckoning us forward. Let us make this year a good year, a year of progress, of development, or spiritual maturing. It will not be without cost to our self-complacent beings, but it will be worth it.

Along the Way

20 JANUARY

DO YOU LISTEN?

DO You listen, Master, when people pray?
Do You hear what they say to You?
Every single voice that rises from the four corners of the earth
in infinite tongues at all hours of the day and night,
do You listen to it all?

Did You catch the wonderful phrase in that man's prayer today?
He addressed You as: 'O effulgent Majesty'.
Do You like to be called 'effulgent Majesty'?
Then he told You the news of the day:
was it news to You?

Sometimes, Lord, a very sobering thought strikes me,
that You don't listen at all to what people are saying
in their very long and wordy prayers,
filled with well-oiled, rolling phrases,
all of a pattern as it was in the beginning.

I'm almost afraid to follow my thought through to its natural sequence.
For, Master, if You don't listen to our words,
but only read our hearts and minds, our hidden longings and desires,
then what we say and what we pray might be poles apart.
And that thought makes me tremble.

When did I last pray to You, really pray,
my stumbling words the imperfect vehicle of my soul's searching,
my silence the awe of worship in Your presence?
Lord, I have need of You just now.
Teach me to pray,
truly pray.

Just a Moment, Lord

AN AWFUL DAY

TODAY, Lord, has been awful!
>It started badly.
Imps of depression sat on the bedposts
>waiting for me to wake,
>ready to pounce on me,
>to harry me
>and fill me with their gloom.

My head ached, my nerves were edgy
>and I felt irritable.

And then it rained . . .
not a decent sort of rain, soon over and done with,
but a penetrating, miserable, drooling kind of rain
that wet-blanketed soul as well as body.

There are days like that, Master.
Days when life is heavy, boring, meaningless;
days when no ray pierces the inward gloom,
>just plain bad days.

What is Your recipe for such hours, Lord?
I am reminded of some words which were often on Your lips:
>'Take heart!'
They must have comforted Your followers many times.
You used them when they were startled,
>when they had lost their nerve,
>when they needed encouragement.

I need encouragement, Master,
so I quieten my mind and wait to hear You say:
>'Take heart!'
Thank You, Lord.

Just a Moment, Lord

IF ONLY I HADN'T

I HAVE a silly habit which annoys me. If I just miss a bus I reason to myself, 'If only I hadn't gone back to shut the garden gate . . . or make sure the door was double-locked . . . or stopped to greet my neighbour . . . I should have caught the bus.' Sometimes I can work backwards over the last half-hour and discover a dozen things I could have done more quickly, or omitted to do, which would have ensured me catching the earlier bus. It is such a waste of time to travel back in thought over the possibilities of having acted otherwise, that I get quite cross with myself. In contrast, if I just catch a bus, I never stop to work out what fortuitous events led to such a happy coincidence.

But I always say in my heart: 'Thank You, Lord.'

Along the Way

A PERFECT DAY

I WANT to thank You for a perfect day, Lord.
Everything has gone right,
every single little thing, as well as the big things.
There was sunshine this morning, with tiny white clouds
sailing across the blue heavens,
the dewy flowers laughed at me as I walked down the
garden path,
and roses wafted their delicious scent in my direction.

Heavenly Father, when You planned Your world,
why did You make it so breathtakingly beautiful?
It hurts, Lord, so much beauty hurts.
It makes a pain inside that is a pain of joy,
a quivering, glowing, lovely little pain
that bursts into the heart and fills it.

I hardly dare to live in Your world when You show its
splendours.
It is too big for me, too marvellous.
But into the small world of my home I fit.
There I can be myself,
and the hours alone are not hours of loneliness, except at times.

Today, though, joy has filled my heart.
African violets nodded to me from the window sill,
and the radio played such happy tunes that I
danced
across the floor as I dusted,
which resulted in very skimpy dusting, Lord.
But You understand, don't You?

I was too happy to bother about such trifles as specks of dust,
so thank You.
Thank You a thousand times for this happy day.
Good night.

Just a Moment, Lord

I CAN'T PRAY

YOUR servant, the apostle, Lord, told us always to pray
        but I can't . . .
        I simply can't
I'm not made that way.
        My mind wanders,
        my foot twitches,
        and I remember, Lord.

Remember that I have to fetch the washing in,
        that I promised to phone Mrs Farley,
        that I forgot to buy flour yesterday,
        and many other things.
        Many, many other things.
So You understand, Master, that it is difficult for me to pray.

Would You mind if I just chatted to You about everything
        while it is happening?
In that way, Lord, I could keep in contact with You.
I could tell You of the things that worry me,
        the things that puzzle me,
        the things I detest
        and the things I enjoy.

And my longings, Master, the deep, deep longings
        that You Yourself have planted in my heart.

It may not be the highest kind of prayer,
it may not be what others can offer You,
        but it will be my way of praying,
        and I believe that You will understand
        and accept it.

Just a Moment, Lord

TANGIBLE PRAYERS

AS I expect you do, I often pray for a person whose name suddenly comes to my mind, but I am trying to follow up such thought-prayers by something tangible – like a letter, or personal – like a phone call. Prayer alone must surely accomplish something, but there is nothing like the comfort of a letter which one can read many times over, or pop under the pillow at night where it gives a sense of friendly care and interest.

Along the Way

SOMEONE TO LISTEN

MASTER, the world is in a hurry,
 from morning till night,
 working, running, talking,
 busy with a thousand things.
No one has time to listen to me,
and I need to talk.

I have so much to say.
Not only small talk about everyday affairs,
 but about deeper things.
I need time to explain how I feel within me,
 the strange longings,
 the disturbing doubts,
 the questionings and probings,
 the hurts I suffer.

I don't only live on the surface, Lord.
There's a lot going on behind my quiet mien.
 Things hard to speak about,
 unless someone will listen,
 really listen to me.
 But no one has time.

So it is all bottled up within my breast,
until at times I feel that I shall burst
 with the inward pressure.

Can I talk to You, Master?
Will You listen patiently
 if my words falter at times,
 if I find it hard to explain myself?
It will bring such relief if I can pour it all out to You,
 for You understand.

With a whole universe to govern,
You have yet time for each single soul.

Thank You, Lord!
I'm sitting at Your feet now,
and You are listening,
so I begin my tale . . .

Just a Moment, Lord

17

THOSE AGGRESSIVE POSTERS

IT'S not like in Your days, Master.
The streets of Nazareth were not plastered with advertisements.
      Loud, aggressive posters.
      Subtle, persuasive posters –
      buy this;
      use that;
      drink the other.

It stimulates the appetite, Lord.
      It creates a want,
        a need,
        an urge,
        to possess,
     to be with it,
     to live on a level with the Joneses.

Life is complex in our days, Master.
Shall we walk with eyes averted
studying the paving stones,
the bits of rubbish in the gutter?
Or shall we walk with upturned gaze
      peering at the clouds chased by the wind?

What other solution is there?
      To learn to say 'No' to these enticements?
      But 'No' is a hard word.
      Hard to say, but harder still to mean.
Your servant Paul said he had learnt to be content
      with what he had,
     which wasn't very much at times.
Perhaps You would help me to learn that lesson too,
and thus save me from falling into snares set by skilful
     salesmen.

Just a Moment, Lord

SAVE ££££s!

HOW easy it is to save money these days! My eye was caught by an advertisement from one firm offering great savings on household goods. Being the happy owner of a new adult toy known as a pocket calculator, I decided to see how much I could save on 10 items. Believe it or not, it was a magnificent £105.45! But wait, to achieve that saving I had to do some buying. Tip, tap, on the calculator went my fingers, adding up what I would have to spend in order to save. The result was a staggering £295.95. Nearly £300! And I could live quite happily without any of the goods advertised. I decided the best saving was not to spend.

Along the Way

A GLAD SPENDTHRIFT

I WANT to be a spendthrift, Lord,
    a spendthrift of my time and strength,
    giving instead of withholding,
    sowing instead of wanting to reap.
Don't let me be a miser, Master,
    cuddling myself to myself,
    careful of every effort,
    counting each step,
    hoarding my physical resources
for the demands of a tomorrow that might never come.

Make me a glad spendthrift, Lord:
    joyously giving my love and care,
    opening the sluice-gates of my small reserves,
    pouring out what little I have to give
    without measure or stint,
    without anxious debate,
    and trusting You for tomorrow.

Don't let me shelter myself in a glass case,
    fearful lest the light of day should fade me,
    dreading that the hand of time should touch me,
    shrinking from effort that might drain me,
    saving myself up . . . for what?
    To look nice in my coffin?

Let me give what I have to give with open hands,
offering myself to You each day for service,
happy to be used as long as life shall last,
living for You as a glad spendthrift.
    For at the end, Lord,
    You will not ask me what I have saved,
    but what I have given.

Just a Moment, Lord

COURAGE TO LIVE

LORD, give me courage to live!
A cheerful courage, Master, if that might be.
Let me wear a smile even when my heart trembles;
let laughter-lines form round my eyes,
and let me hold my chin up
and go forward.

Lord, give me courage to live!
A grim, unsmiling courage, if need be.
Courage to face the empty days,
        unfulfilled hopes,
        black hours,
        defeats, maybe;
a hard, defiant courage, that will hang on until things are better.
        Grant me that, Lord.

Master, give me courage to live!
Your servant Sangster wrote that 'in the dark,
        brave souls hold on to the skirts of God'.
Give me courage like that, Lord,
        clinging courage, desperate courage,
        that will not let You go.
If feeling goes, if faith goes, if fortitude fails,
        let me just hold on, clinging to You,
        knowing that You are there,
        counting on You to see me through.

Just a Moment, Lord

NOT ME!

AT about 17 years of age I had my photo taken to give to some friends in exchange for theirs. Sepia colour was the rage at that time. What to wear was a problem but I finally decided on a jumper I had knitted myself in a lacy pattern. For me, facing a camera is as bad as facing a dentist, so I had to pluck up courage to call at the studio. When I went to collect the photos, I stared in disbelief. 'That's not me!' I said with conviction to the lady photographer, and I remember with a shudder her reply: 'Of course it is!' Crushed, but convinced by the evidence of my handmade jumper, I paid up and left her shop, hating myself more than ever. Now when I look at it, the photo is quite nice, but at the time it was a nasty shock!

Along the Way

SNOWDROPS

MASTER, You walked along sun-baked roads
    with bare feet in sandals,
possibly choosing the shade of trees for comfort.
Yet some of the nights were chilly,
when it was good to wrap up in a cloak.
We of the north know a harsher winter
and our 'sandal days' are limited to brief summer,
so how eagerly we welcome any sign
    of an early spring.

One cold winter day I saw the snowdrops.
Not in a garden, no, and certainly
    not in my own.
They grew in a zinc pail
    in a concreted yard.
A half-dozen or so of the delicate flowers
    hung their green-white bells
    among a duster of small weeds.

The metal pail and the concrete base
had concentrated what warmth there was
    to bring an early flowering.

As I walked past I said again, 'Thank You, Lord!'
    – a very frequent phrase of mine –
    but it was heartfelt.
We humans need the small encouragements
    along the way;
a flower here, a smile or handshake there,
    a friendly word with a neighbour.
These are not earth-shaking happenings
    but they have real importance
in cheering us along our daily pathway.
So I repeat: Thank You, Lord, for snowdrops.

My God and I

ACCEPT YOURSELF

WE have to live with ourselves so we must accept ourselves as we are. Recognise our weak points. Be humbly happy over our good points, for surely we have one or two if we look hard enough to find them.

Hints for Living

THE HAT

PEOPLE get in the way, Lord,
      when I am trying to think about You in church;
      trying to make spiritual contact,
      to open my heart and to worship You.
Suddenly I am aware of a large hat
      right in front of my eyes,
      a large aggressive hat blocking my vision.
I dodge it to catch a glimpse of the altar,
I squeeze to right and lean to left
but the hat remains impenetrable.

What is even worse is that it becomes dominant in my
                thoughts.
Forgetting the altar I concentrate on the hat . . .
      and its wearer, yes, its wearer.
Who does she think she is, blocking my view like that?

I preen myself with a good conscience.
      My hat isn't as big as that;
      I am discreet, thoughtful of others, even in that detail.

Suddenly I realise what is happening.
      My intent to worship has vanished,
      my spiritual desires have cooled, I am hot and irritated.

In Your very house I am fighting a losing battle,
      all because of a hat.
Lord, it is ridiculous that such a thing can shut You out
      and wake unpleasant feelings within me.
My desire to meet with You, to worship You,
      must be stronger than that.
I must see You with my inward eyes right through all barriers.
Help me to do just that, Master,
and also make me a little wiser where I sit next time.

Between You and Me, Lord

THE LONG, RED TONGUE

WHEN I was in the first class at school, some of the children had been talking too much and the teacher hit on a novel idea for punishing offenders. On several sheets of brown paper she drew a long, red tongue, sticking them together until the tongue measured about a metre in length. Then, fixing the class with a stern eye she said, 'The very next child who speaks without permission will come out here in front of the class and stand with this tongue pinned to her clothes.'

Sure enough, moments later a child forgot the awful warning and chatted happily to her neighbour. Forward to the front she must go, and stand wearing the long, red tongue. It was then I became aware that my tongue had something to do with my power of speech.

I have often thought of that unfortunate child standing in front of the class with the long, red tongue hanging in front. It has always reminded me of Jesus' words:

'But I tell you that men will have to give account on the day of judgement for every careless word they have spoken' (Matthew 12:36, *NIV*).

Ur Minnets Gömmor (Down Memory Lane)

SUN OR SHADE?

MASTER, You often walked amid throngs of people
so You would have felt at home in the High Street this morning.
I stared in wonder at the dense mass of slowly moving shoppers,
      realising what was special about them.
On what was otherwise a cold wintry day
      they were all walking, tightly packed,
      on the sunny pavement across the road.
From where I was in the chilly shade
the picture the sunlit strollers presented was most attractive.
I wished I could have joined them,
but the shops I sought lay on the shady side, so I must stay there.

Had I been given the choice, Lord,
I should have opted for the sunshine,
      the warmth and brightness
      across the way.
It is so natural to choose the sunny side,
      the easy path,
      the pleasant scenery.
But life does not always give me the choice!
Sometimes I am forced into the shadows and
      the cold winds quite against my inclination.
But as I take the path of duty into the chill of the shade
let me remember that the sun is still shining
even if its warming rays do not for the moment
      reach me.

My God and I

IT'S A FACT!

HOW often people assert, 'It's a fact!' to back up some statement they have made.

Recently I have been cogitating over the difference between facts and their interpretation. People may agree on the bare outline of essential facts yet disagree fundamentally in interpreting what has happened.

And that is the cause of a lot of unrest, of enmity and even war.

Between husband and wife there can be vastly different reactions to the same set of circumstances, and try getting a couple of children to explain who started the fight!

We all see matters from our own personal angle and interpret facts accordingly. We know we are right because we have seen it with our own eyes, heard it with our own ears. One man went back to America recently and reported that England no longer had any sands round its coasts. He had seen it with his own eyes.

It did not occur to him that he had seen the coast at high tide and that a few hours would have changed his view and therefore his viewpoint.

Next time we hotly affirm, 'It's a fact!' let us try to remember that there might be more than our own interpretation of that fact.

Along the Way

WINTER MORNING

THERE was washing to do, Master,
    but I didn't feel like it.
    Anyway, it wasn't urgent.
I wandered out to the garden –
    into the chill raw air
in the hope of finding some early buds.

My startled gaze fell on some periwinkles,
    both white and blue.
It didn't seem long since I had planted them,
hardly long enough for them to flower.
Then the grass took my attention,
    not the grass
    where it should be, in the lawn,
but the flourishing tufts in the flower-beds.

I fetched a hoe and started to work.
Suddenly I realised that some birds were chirping,
      hidden from me in nearby trees.
Their song was one of mirth and gaiety,
certainly not reflecting the poor weather.

With lighter heart I plied my task
then after half an hour I gave up,
      not tired but invigorated.
I marched indoors and soon had the washing machine
        purring,
      then I cleaned the kitchen and did some cooking,
      feeling jubilant with my progress.
What delightful surprises You had in reserve for me,
      Lord,
      on that dull winter morning.
      Thank You!

Towards You, Lord

CONQUEST

WHAT a lovely feeling one gets after having completed a disagreeable but necessary task! It is almost as though an aura of conquest quivers around one's head and little joybells tinkle in the heart.

Such a happy feeling I got after a desperate attack on the dandelions in my lawn. There they crouched, malevolent in their animosity, looking as ferocious as the predatory crown of thorns in Australian waters, flattened against the ground where the lawnmower could not touch them. Day after day they mocked me until it dawned on me that I could eradicate them one by one.

I felt a sense of release, even triumph. I planned a modest target of at least a dozen plants dug out per day. The first two days I exceeded my self-set ration of work, and on the third day – when I could really see that I was making progress against the enemy encroachment – I decided to go all out and finish the job.

The halo round my head when I finished must have been visible from afar. I could almost imagine a band playing: 'See the conquering hero comes . . .' How glad I was that I had taken action instead of moaning and groaning daily about something that could be changed with a little time and effort.

Along the Way

THE 'I KNOW' PEOPLE

LORD, deliver me from the 'I know' people!
  'I know what you want . . .
  I know how you feel . . .
  I know what you should do . . .'

Master, they don't know!
  How can they?
They are not me, in my circumstances,
with my temperament and talents . . . and failings.

That man in the shop.
I can still see his triumphant smile:
  'I've got exactly what you want.'
  He hadn't!
He hadn't even grasped what I was seeking.

The woman in the bus:
  'I know how you feel . . .'
A rainy morning, a heavy cold, tired feet,
yes, there were all those ingredients,
but what did she know of the letter I'd received:
  the crushing of hopes,
  anxiety for a loved one,
  happy plans now spoiled?

Lord, give me patience with the 'I know' people.
Let me recognise their goodwill
  and would-be helpfulness,
and let me express my gratitude
  at least with a generous smile
  and a pleasant word.

Towards You, Lord

PEOPLE LEAN ON ME

PEOPLE lean on me, Master.
  Lean heavily,
And I don't want to be leaned on.
I myself want to lean on someone else
  for support,
  for comfort,
  for understanding,
  for approval.

So what am I to do, Lord, when people lean on me
    for sympathy,
    for strength,
    for love,
    for prayers?

One has to be strong to be leaned on
    and I am not strong, Master,
    not in myself.
I need a new infusion of Your power.

Can You so undergird and stabilise me
that I can bear up against these leanings and
offer myself as a wall of strength
    to those with trembling limbs?

Will You take away my own desire
    to lean on others,
and teach me to lean only on You, dear Lord?
    In that way I could be strong,
for Your strength and courage would flow into my heart
    and through me out to others.
    Then when they leaned on me
    I should not fail them,
    for I should be leaning hard on You.

Just a Moment, Lord

11 FEBRUARY

LOVING YOURSELF (2)

IF we don't like ourselves enough to be happy in our own company as often as necessary, then something is wrong. No change of place or work or companions will change the picture except momentarily, for we carry our difficulties within ourselves.

Many of us, if we could choose, would be different from what we are. Most blond people wish they were dark, the brunettes dream of a gloria of golden hair. In these days it is simple to have the hair dyed if one wants, but dyed hair does not change the tint of the skin and the colour of the eyes. It usually gives an artificial look.

We are all more or less self-conscious about how we look. For the older woman it is a bit of a trial to see herself in the glass each morning and note that she hasn't grown any younger. But when I speak about liking oneself, I mean the inward personality, the person behind the outward face, the *real* you.

Hints for Living

PEN AND PAPER

IT'S astonishing, Master,
what therapeutic value lies in writing,
        getting it out of the system
        by putting it on paper.

The desire for self-expression
        need not demand advanced art,
        complicated and meaningless patterns,
        bizarre colours and shapes
        or phraseology so obscure as to baffle.
We can just write as we feel at the moment.

A sheet of paper and a pen . . .
such simple means can sometimes do more to ease
            stress
        than a day's holiday.
Help me to remember this, Lord,
        and practise it when necessary.

At times when I'm feeling perplexed
        or angry or sad,
let me write in ordinary words what I feel
        and if possible why I feel so.

No other eyes save Yours need see the result
        for I can destroy it at once,
but the very tabulating of my troubles
and their possible solutions
        will bring relief
        and perhaps greater clarity.

Lord, help me to be wise enough to use this simple
            means
        of lessening some of life's strain.

Between You and Me, Lord

DON'T WEAR A HALO

THIS was just a piece of light-hearted fun I heard on the radio. 'Don't wear a halo, for it is just one more thing to keep clean.'

We were also reminded that a halo needs to slip less than 12 inches to become a noose.

Along the Way

IS THIS LOVE?

LORD, I *must* talk to You.
That young man I met yesterday bowled me over.
I've never felt like that before.
It seemed that an invisible cord drew us together
and when our eyes met, something magnetic happened.
      At least it did to me.
I thrilled, I responded with all my being;
      suddenly I was happy.

I wondered if he felt the same but I couldn't tell.
      A little later he had to leave
      and I felt such a vacuum.
Friends continued to chat
      but it meant nothing to me
      for my thoughts were elsewhere.

Is this real love, Master?
This sudden quickening of interest in a stranger,
this increase in the pulse's tempo?

Can it happen to one of two
      and not to the other?
Today I'm wondering.

What do I know of this young man except his name
      and that my heart responded to him at once?
Was it merely physical attraction,
      or a deeper call from the spirit?

Lord, it is a relief to open my heart to You
      for at this stage I can tell no other.
I don't want to make any mistake in this important matter
      of falling in love.
I can't control what I feel
      but I can control the expression of those feelings.
      Do help me, Master.
      I need You urgently just now.

Towards You, Lord

STAND UP AND BE COUNTED

LIFE challenges us many times to 'stand up and be counted', even though it is far easier to stifle one's inward convictions and to go with the crowd. My first taste of showing my colours was of a political nature, strange to say. Just after I started in a certain school there was a voting campaign in our town in which even we children became involved. We wore the colours of 'our' party, or rather of our parents' party.

It was rather frightening at first to leave home with a coloured rosette pinned to the coat, not knowing how many others would be like-minded. Once at school we formed into bands shouting party slogans and insults at the opposite group. Actual fighting did not take place but we came very near it. As I remember it now, it seemed rather thrilling to show one's colours.

Some years later I learned to 'stand up and be counted' for God, when I took my decision to be his follower.

It is quite modern to wear a badge, a slogan on a sweatshirt, or some other insignia to indicate which club or group you belong to. Usually there is no special bravery required. But to show your allegiance to Christ sometimes requires courage. Paul wrote to the Romans (1:16), 'I am not ashamed of the gospel.' He probably did not wear a badge on his clothes but his whole life spoke for his Master and witnessed of his power. May we, too, show the same courage in our day and generation.

Ur Minnets Gömmor (Down Memory Lane)

NOT GOOD ENOUGH

MASTER, I feel Your censure over my life:
    good, but not good enough,
    warm, but not glowing,
    shallow instead of deep,
    casual instead of committed,
    indifferent instead of involved,
    soft instead of sturdy.

What can I do about it, Lord? What is wrong?
Does self sit too securely in the saddle?
Is it body-tiredness, mental strain,
    or has it a deeper cause?
Is it the looseness of a rubber band at rest,
    or of one that has lost its stretch?
Is it the long slow decline into the valley of age?
    Passing or permanent?

You see, Lord, what a lot of questions I ask You,
and yet I don't really need any answers.
All I require is new contact with You,
        a quickening,
        a refreshing,
        a renewal.
Then I shall be able to continue.

Meet with me, Master, just now,
stretch out Your hand and I will stretch out mine . . . There!
Now I can go on.

Just a Moment, Lord

DRAB DAYS

WHAT a day it's been, Lord, just plain drab!
No flash of colour, of excitement, of anticipation,
no joy from the past, no hope for the future,
only flat, grey monotony today.
The weather was dull and I was dull, everyone else seemed dull.
How can life change so suddenly from major to minor key?
Not a plaintive haunting minor which has a charm all its own,
        but a toneless, repetitive, boring sequence.
Not even the birds were chirping.
They huddled together on bare branches,
        wet feathers not improving their appearance,
        looking as miserable as I felt.

The scientists have an explanation of such depression, Master;
        one's bio-rhythms are at their lowest ebb.
It's all very well for them to plan their charts,
        it's infinitely more difficult to live through the cycles.

All right, I'll accept their explanation!
If I'm at the bottom of the curves today,
        then I shall be in the ascendant tomorrow.
        That's certainly a cheering thought.
Roll on, heavy hours, and up with you, my bio-rhythms,
        tomorrow will be better.
I really believe it, Lord, for my spirits are rising even now.
        Thank You for that.

Between You and Me, Lord

LOVER'S TIFF

IT was all his fault, Lord!
He deliberately aggravated me
    when he knew I was feeling down.
He knows that I dislike that green tie
    so he wore it to annoy me,
and he called me 'kid'
    as though I wasn't grown up.
I'm simply seething with rage.

I admit that I flared up too quickly.
After a difficult day at work
    my nerves were on edge.
I needed soothing, not irritating;
I wanted him to take me in his arms
    telling me how much he loved me.
Instead of which he teased me. I blazed at him
    and flounced out of the room,
    telling him to go home.

I'm miserable, Master, near to tears,
    but it really was his fault,
    well, most of it;
    at least some of it.
I suppose I was touchy,
and perhaps he wasn't his best self.
I wonder if he'll phone to say he's sorry?
Perhaps *I* should phone first . . .
    but that would be hard to do.

Help me, Lord, to conquer my pride
    and forget my hurt.
It probably was mostly my fault . . .

Give me grace to say so and to take the blame.
    It's hard, though . . .
Here goes, Master. *With Your help* I'll do it.
    I'll call his number
and bring this lover's tiff to an end.

Towards You, Lord

MY JEWISH SCHOOL-FRIEND

DURING my childhood my parents moved from town to town. It was often exciting, yet to start a new school, in a new part of the country where the dialect is different, can be agony to a sensitive child.

In one school in the north of England I was very unhappy. The girls made fun of me, of my southern accent and ways. They were already a clique of close friends and I was left outside. These months were some of the hardest of my school years. But there were two bright spots during the first term. An understanding form-mistress who taught us literature – my favourite subject – and a Jewish classmate.

This girl was the only one to befriend me in the beginning. She would come up to me in the lunch hour to say a few friendly words. I had no idea at the beginning that she was Jewish. I only knew that she was absent from class each time we had Scripture lessons.

Then one day our form-mistress announced it was the Jewish Passover, and we might be interested to hear Mary tell us about Jewish customs. Mary had brought along with her some unleavened bread which she broke into small pieces and let us taste, and she explained how the Passover supper was still observed in her own home.

I listened in amazement. I knew it all from the Bible, of course, after many years in Sunday school. But to think that it was still practised – that thought had not occurred to me before.

My friend, Mary, was one of God's chosen people, the Jews. It was almost as though I saw a halo round her head. My excitement grew when our teacher told us that it was generally believed that the priestly tribe of Aaron had chestnut (red) hair. And Mary had deep auburn hair! How the Bible came alive for me that day! It was no longer a history book of long ago. It breathed, it glowed, it lived.

In my heart I have always been grateful to Mary who befriended an unhappy school-mate. But I am also grateful to her because she made an old religious custom live for me and by that means brought God nearer to my consciousness.

Ur Minnets Gömmor (Down Memory Lane)

WANDERING THOUGHTS

LESLIE WEATHERHEAD gave some good advice about the problem of wandering thoughts in prayer time: 'Sometimes it is a good thing to note just where they do wander, to ask why they wander there, and to pray about the situation to which they drift.'

Along the Way

TELEVISION CLOSE-UP PRAYERS

AT times it is unnerving when the television picture zooms in on a close-up. Sometimes the faces are frightening, sometimes distasteful. At times they are most attractive. I think children's faces are very lovely and quite naturally I find myself praying for the youngsters. 'God bless that girl . . . help that boy to grow into a good man.'

The last time I watched the Moscow State Circus, a lovely family group was in the close-ups. Instinctively I prayed for them, sending out God's love and blessing over them. Then it occurred to me that the recorded programme had taken place long before, so what was the use of praying about any of it?

Pondering the matter I came to the conclusion that God could use prayers forwards or backwards in time, across distance and language barriers. I believe that when we pray for people we help to create a climate of goodwill and love around them which God can use for their benefit. So I go on praying for the faces that I notice on my screen.

Along the Way

THE WHEEL OF DUTY

I'M bound to the wheel of duty, Master;
it whirls round, carrying me in its dizzy turnings.
    I long at times for freedom but must go on.
    I say, 'Stop', but it doesn't stop.
    I say, 'Can't' . . .
    but I find I can because I must.

Lord, my hands hold precious things;
eternal truths are on my lips,
very often on my lips;
    and I'm afraid.

    Afraid of becoming mechanical.
    Afraid of talking for the sake of talking,
    repeating a lesson well learned.
    Playing a part
    with my thoughts elsewhere,
    my interest elsewhere.

Don't let me become a machine, Lord,
    however well adapted,
    however effective,
    however productive.

Help me to give myself with my message,
        some of myself in everything I do:
And when pressure is heavy and the programme packed,
        come to me with some special grace.

        Let me link on to Your strength,
        let me rest in Your love,
        let me remain a tool in Your hands
        and not become a self-propelling gadget.

Lord, I'm afraid: afraid of becoming a machine.
        Only You can help me.
        Come to me now.
        Touch me into new awareness of Your presence;
        let me remain a channel of Your love,
        an instrument for Your use,
        not a robot.

Just a Moment, Lord

23 FEBRUARY

SHORTAGES

LORD, gloom is in the air
        prophets of doom abound.
The world is running short of
        vital products;
Its natural resources are being depleted
        at a rapid rate.
We are living above our means,
drawing heavily on the few pounds we still have
        in the energy bank.

At such a time, Master, it is good
        to remind ourselves
that Your spiritual resources are limitless.
Your bounties are immeasurable,
        Your love all-embracing.
It gives such inward security to know
        that if all else fails,
        You do not fail.
If all else goes, *You remain.*

Thank You, Lord, for that certainty
Which can keep my heart at peace,
        cradled in Your care.

From My Treasure Chest

TOO MUCH

I FEEL I have too much, Lord!
    Too much of good things.
Out of the pale blue sky the sun shines
    through my windows,
while frost crystals sparkle on the grass.
A pleasant warmth surrounds me indoors.
I am well clad to maintain comfort
    and to save energy
which for most of us means to save expense!
I raise my heart to You in thanksgiving
when suddenly this feeling of 'too much'
    overwhelms me.

Yes, I have had my troubles and my sorrows,
    my problems and my pains,
but just now all is well. I am at peace
    within and without.
It almost seems too much!

I make that feeling the basis of my prayer.
    Thank You, Lord,
    thank You for everything.
Grant that the smooth tenor of my present lot
may lead me nearer You in deep gratitude,
and may my heart be more open to those
    less fortunate than I.

God in My Everyday

GOLDEN SPRING

O GOD, how liberally You clothe the world in yellow,
    particularly in spring!
After winter's greyness and chill
You brush Your yellow tones over the drab countryside,
    in blazing points of golden light.
How beautiful is Your world in springtime!

Coltsfoot flowers hug the brown earth closely,
    as yet unshielded by leaves.
Forsythia decorates the bushes while daffodils
    flaunt their trumpets in the breeze,

and dandelions peep cheekily up from the grass.
Over the moors the gorse flames into colour
while pale primroses cuddle shyly near the hedges.
Breathtakingly lovely is Your world!

Parting the clouds the sun emerges
      bolder for every day;
the golden sunlight filters through in cascades
      of shining warmth.
How my heart responds to springtime, Lord!
Not only do all my senses rejoice
      but in my heart there is
      a golden ray of new hope,
      kindled by Your love.
Winter is past; my flagging spirits revive.
I am conscious of Your nearness . . .
      Thank You, Lord.

God in My Everyday

26 FEBRUARY

THE END OF THE WORLD

CHILDREN pick up strange bits of adult conversation. I was only a child starting in elementary school when I heard that which made me shiver. I did not dare to ask for further details as the subject scared me too much.

The brief phrases I heard were, 'They are trying to split the atom and if they succeed the world will come to an end. Everything will fall to pieces.' What the atom was, and who 'they' were who were trying to split it, I did not reflect upon. The world – *my* world – would come to an end. I would ponder this as I walked to school. 'Everything would fall to pieces'. I tried to imagine what that would mean and I trembled.

Sometimes this fear sat upon my pillow at night and I shivered with apprehension to think that even at that very moment perhaps 'they' might have found the secret they sought and that by morning my world would be no more. What would happen to *me*?

One can smile indulgently as one looks back over childish terrors, but they were very real then. What I did not know, what no one knew, was that inside the atom, once they succeeded in splitting it, they would find a new infinitesimal world to explore.

It is not only children who are afraid of death. Many adults feel a strange, cold terror at the thought of this unknown experience. There is nothing to fear! Could the unborn child know it had to face the ordeal of birth into this world, how it would shrink from it. Yet loving hands received it and cared for it.

I am convinced that something like this will happen to each one of us as we step over the border. Why should we not look forward with joyous anticipation?

Ur Minnets Gömmor (Down Memory Lane)

27 FEBRUARY

HANG-ON FAITH

LORD, grant me faith, faith in You,
    in Your purposes,
    in Your wisdom and Your power,
    but above all, in Your love.
I would have faith as a resplendent lamp,
    glowing in darkness, lighting my path.
I would have faith as an endless treasure,
    from which to draw for daily needs.
I would have faith for total commitment to You,
    to live daily in childlike unconcern.
But, Master, my faith is only a grim hang-on faith,
    battered and worn by many conflicts,
    gripped tightly in my clutching fingers.
I dare not let it go, and yet it is so small!

It is my link with You, my vital link with You.
If I lose it, the gloom of doubt will close in upon me,
    the darkness of despair will cloud my steps.
I must hold fast to it, my tiny scrap of faith.
Sometimes I think I have lost it,
then a word from Your Book, a comment from a friend,
    or a line from a well-known hymn,
revives the near-extinguished flame.

I can't tell people how near I am to unbelief,
how cold doubt chills me until I almost give up,
how what I once accepted as true seems at times
    as empty fable and false hope.
But to You, Master, I confess my doubts as I pray:
    'Help my unbelief.'
Yet through it all, in my hard-clenched fist,
I shelter this spark of faith left to me,
    this hang-on faith.
May it never be wrested from my grasp.

Towards You, Lord

ENGAGED

I'm engaged! But what does that mean?
A telephone can be 'engaged' one moment
    and free the next,
but surely not a person, not a *real* person?
Lord, help me to realise what I have done.
I have plighted my troth, my love and loyalty,
    to a fine young man.

Does he really want me to share his life?
This comparative stranger . . . how shall I live with him?
We don't really know each other in depth.
Oh, we know the outside, the way we look and dress,
    the smiles, the loving glances.
We're on our best behaviour with each other as yet
but our fears and weaknesses, our shortcomings,
we keep locked within our own breasts.

We must break down these barriers before we marry;
    talk freely to each other.
Will our love survive the ordeal of early breakfast
    and the rush to work?
Will it outlast the off-moments that each one has,
    nature's dark side showing through?
Will it last through sunshine and storm,
    through youth and up to old age?

It must, Lord! It *will,* Master, with Your help.
As we take this step together we bow before You,
    acknowledging our need of You.
Lay Your hand upon our heads,
You Who have given us the gift of mutual love,
    Expand and deepen it,
so that the buffeting winds of life
will only serve to strengthen the roots which bind us together.
Looking up into Your face, Master,
we believe we see Your approving smile.

Towards You, Lord

29 FEBRUARY
SAINTS

YOU want to make us saints, Master?
Isn't that rather a barren hope,
a pinnacle of achievement too far away in the clouds
            to be feasible?

Me, a saint?
With my temperament, my weaknesses, failings
            and contradictions?
You're joking, Lord!
You know the ingredients of my personality,
all I have inherited from my forbears of good
            and less good
and, to be quite frank, of evil.

You set the standard too high, Lord,
and You won't leave me in peace.
            You pull and push,
            nudge and prod.
You prune and discipline and train
to raise me to a higher spiritual level,
and I am like a recalcitrant donkey, kicking,
            plunging and resisting.

Why do You continue to bother with me?
Honestly, Master, the heights of holiness do call me,
I feel their attraction, their challenge,
            but I am way down in the valley
            and the snowy heights are distant.
Don't despair of me, Master.
Don't yield to my obstinacy and leave me alone.
Keep working at me, believing for me,
            leading me upwards.
Don't get a halo ready for me just yet,
            for it wouldn't fit.
Let me struggle and endure and aspire,
and one day I pray I may win through.

Towards You, Lord

FACING BOTH WAYS

LIFE is difficult, Master.
There seem to be two sides to every question,
        differing paths to each goal,
and I am caught in the middle facing both ways.

There is the tug between body and soul
            action and prayer,
            material and spiritual values,
            self-denial and self-fulfilment.
They are two sides of one reality,
and seemingly battling for supremacy
            with me clamped in the centre,
my feelings oscillating between them.

Give me guidance, Lord, on how to balance my life,
        to use it to best advantage.
As I hesitate between alternatives,
        direct my thinking,
lead me to the right decision and help me to follow it through.
If I have Your approval it will be easier to bear criticism.

Make me strong against the self-doubt that arises,
the questionings: would it be wise?
        would it be misinterpreted?
If in a moment of insight I see my way,
let me follow it when the clouds descend
        and cold mists envelop me.
The momentary hesitation over, let me step forth
        in faith that You are leading me
        in the right way.

God in My Everyday

MAN'S TWO SELVES

PAUL TOURNIER wrote that in each of us are two selves, the one presented
to the world and the hidden true self. In the struggle to integrate these two
selves man finds the real adventure of living. We all know our outer self that
we feed, wash, clothe and often pamper, but our inner self is an unknown
mystery of very contrary cross currents. Our friends (and enemies!) know
the self we present to the world, but only God knows our inner true self and
only he can bring the adjustments and integration necessary to make us
whole and harmonious right through.

Along the Way

ACCEPTANCE

LORD, I'm fighting it!
This sequence of events beyond my control.
      It isn't fair, it isn't right!
Everything within me protests,
my hackles rise and my heart thumps in anger,
         yet I can't alter it.

I'm in the grip of a system, Master,
      a cold, hard, callous system,
      a machine that grinds and pulverises
      without thought of personal feelings,
      without caring for circumstances.

I feel like hurling myself against this brick wall
      but it is I who would come to grief
      and not the system.
What shall I do, Lord?

Help me to accept it, Master,
      to swallow this unacceptable mouthful
      even if it nearly chokes me,
      and not to resist it any longer.
Teach me how to live with it,
to wrest any nourishment it might offer
      for mind or soul or character,
      though the very prospect fills me with dismay . . .

You must help me, Lord,
      for the sake of peace within,
so that my body chemistry is not thrown off balance
      by inward aggression
      however well suppressed.

Between You and Me, Lord

PROGRESS

PROGRESS is a funny business, Lord.
It is often one step forward,
      then a slide back again.
One invention cancels out another,
and every new item produced creates a desire for something else,
a desire which becomes a need, a burning need.

What irony that when washing machines
      became customary in most homes,
new textiles were produced that required hand-wash.
No sooner were thermostatic irons popular
      than non-iron fabrics appeared.
Following the acquisition of a spin-drier,
      one resents the label: 'Do not spin'
      on the new purchases.
We are kept in a perpetual state of expecting
      something different, beyond the present,
and yet we are left unsatisfied.

Spiritual progress is otherwise, Lord,
      for You are in charge there.
You are not always thinking how to outwit us,
      hoodwink us into trying new ways.
Spiritual progress is slow, even unnoticeable
      by the person concerned,
and only You can assess the ground covered
      and the improvement made.
Perhaps our greatest step forward is when we see ourselves
      as we are in Your sight,
which can be a very unnerving experience.
Our greatest comfort is that we are in Your hands,
      and You know the goal to which You are leading us.
Help us to plod on faithfully.

Towards You, Lord

A HA'PORTH OF TAR

MY father had a seemingly inexhaustible fund of sayings and proverbs, many garnered from 15 years as a Salvation Army pioneer officer in Argentina. Over the years he must have given us children lots of good advice, but I only seem to remember the maxims, for they echo in my thoughts and often give me just the guidance or reproof that I need.

'Don't spoil the ship for a ha'porth of tar,' came out when I was trying to economise in time, money or effort on some job or other – probably often needed as I was always trying to find a short cut through.

'The sheep that stops to bleat loses a mouthful,' quietened us when we were a bit too talkative at meal times! On other occasions when I was wondering if I should complain about something I felt was wrong, he guided my thinking with: 'It's the baby that cries that gets fed.'

Along the Way

TO KICK ONESELF

I COULD have kicked myself, Master!
Just after she left me I realised
      what I should have said,
      what I ought to have done
      and how I could have helped.
It was too late for second thoughts, for self-recrimination.
She was speeding away in her car her errand unfulfilled,
      her need still great,
her search still on for someone
who could help her out of a dilemma.

Was I too occupied with my own affairs
      when she called
to respond intuitively to her need?
Was my mind too slow in working,
      my heart too tepid to care,
      my link with You too frail
for You to urge me into quicker response?

This opportunity has passed into oblivion.
I am left 'kicking myself' for my failure.
Perhaps I should stop doing that and instead
      ask You to make me more sensitive
      to others' problems,
and thus more able to come to their aid.

My God and I

SUNNY BANK

MY heart thrilled with pleasure, Lord,
      as I read the name Sunny Bank.
Thank You for that, Master.
I felt it was Your gift to me on that dull wet morning.

I sat in a bus on a shopping trip when the road name
      caught my eye, Sunny Bank!
My mind fought against reality,
that a road with that delightful name could be
      merely a viaduct over a railway, drab, grey and noisy.
I clung to the picture the name conjured up . . .
In thought I saw children gathering primroses in spring,
pouncing eagerly upon the gay flowers in the hedgerows;

couples strolling along the narrow path by the railway siding,
while a leisurely engine puffed slowly past;
families picnicking in the lush grass,
yielding themselves outstretched to the sun's
pleasant warmth.

Pictures from the past when the name Sunny Bank
had been rightly given.
Was it not better, Lord, that I should dwell on those
than on the unpleasing present?

Isn't that Your gift, Master?
Your wondrous glowing gift,
that by imagination we can escape the present to live in
a fairyland of fantasy
for a few brief moments?
My heart felt warmed and happy
and the world seemed a better place.
Thank You, Lord, for Sunny Bank.

Towards You, Lord

8 MARCH

WASHING DEMONSTRATIONS

I AM a bit of a cynic about the marvellous washing demonstrations on TV. The terribly dirty football shorts come up whiter than white when a certain powder is used. I strongly suspect some of the clean shirts and shorts held up for our view have never been worn, let alone soiled.

Long ago I arranged for some washing demonstrations in the home league I was responsible for.

One demonstrator held up pieces of flannel obviously rubbed lightly with some soot. Of course they came up shining white after washing.

We were not impressed.

We wanted a product to take out the worn-in grime on children's shirts and blouses. With another demonstrator we had better luck. She asked for a dozen ladies to give her their neck scarves, which she proceeded to wash and rinse, and then hang on an improvised line between chairs. While they part-dried she gave her talk on the best way of managing the weekly family wash. We listened attentively, with a glance cast now and again at the multi-coloured line of scarves.

Her talk over, the lady produced an electric iron and, with a board between two chairs, ironed out the scarves and redistributed them to their delighted owners. That demonstration convinced us!

Along the Way

RELIEF

WORLD news is bad today, Lord.
The items beat in shock waves upon my mind and heart;
     I felt depressed and hopeless.
Strikes, accidents, bombings, pollution.
What an unending list of disasters!
I lifted my heart to You but I hardly knew what to say
     except: 'Save us or we perish!'

Later I walked into the garden to soothe my feelings.
     What relief it brought me!
There is something magical about growing plants and greenness
     which brings You near, Master.
I see Your handiwork, Your co-operation with man;
I come a little nearer to the secret of life itself
     and I worship You.
A faint spring sunshine drifted from between billowing clouds,
the soil was moist and smelled clean and fresh.
The bad news began to fade from my mind,
     or rather recede into a right perspective.
All was not lost. All was not hopeless.
There was still God . . .
     and His power and His love.

Lord, Your natural laws are still dependable
     and unalterable by any whim or wickedness from man.
This firm conviction took fresh root in my being
     and I felt quieted and poised.
With relief in my heart I turned back to the house.
The announcer was again droning out his bad news
     but I could receive it with more equanimity
for I had been reminded that GOD IS.

Between You and Me, Lord

A COMPULSIVE COMPOSTER

I HAVE become a compulsive composter. Every orange peel is pounced upon from the plates, all potato peelings are saved, fluff from the carpet sweeper is hoarded and they all go on to the compost heap at the end of the garden to make the rich dark mould the plants thrive in. The dustbin is much nearer the kitchen door than the compost heap and sometimes I am tempted, in bad weather, to take the easy way out and put possible composting materials into the dead-end of the dustbin. Then my conscience reads the Riot Act to me. Don't I want lovely rich earth in the garden? Yes, I do! Then I must be willing to go the long hard way down the garden in the pouring rain or the icy wind.

Some people can get quite lyrical about compost heaps. It always appears a miracle to me that you can put decaying stuff on top and shovel out from below the most satisfying handfuls of valuable dark compost to add to your garden soil.

Along the Way

OUT OF BREATH

I'M out of breath, Master, panting, tired and hot,
  yet I haven't stirred from my home.
I've been running a race with myself,
  not using my legs
  but my nerves and thoughts;
getting flustered over small details of daily routine
with my thoughts urging me on in a dozen directions at once.

It's quite senseless, Lord,
  I agree with You there.
But how shall I avoid this inward build-up,
this mounting tension which reaches snapping point
  over insignificant matters?

You are showing me one thing clearly, Master,
that I must not carry tomorrow's load today.
What makes me race is that I am tackling future problems
  while I do today's duties,
tackling them in fussy, fluttering anxiety
  which makes me gasp for breath.

Slow me up in my thoughts, Lord,
  and quicken me up physically.
Am I asking too much?
I want to be alive and spry in my body
  but relaxed and poised in mind,
so that the machinery does not wear out from the inside
  through constant friction.
Teach me to relax, Master,
and grant me some of Your own serenity.

Between You and Me, Lord

12 March

THE GOLDEN RULE FOR COMPOST

THE golden rule for compost appears to be 'Anything that comes from nature can go back to nature to enrich the soil.' Nylons, therefore, are definitely out, but newspapers, if torn up and soaked, can be added to the heap of vegetable waste and garden refuse.

Tea leaves, coffee grounds, lawn mowings, seaweed for those who can get it, fallen leaves – the variety is endless and it is fun to produce your own good garden compost from such waste products. I have even read that it is possible to make compost from an old mattress, but somehow the idea of an ancient mattress dominating the landscape at the end of the garden doesn't appeal to me.

Here's to good composting this year!

Along the Way

13 March

WEEDS AND FLOWERS

THERE is one thing I should like to ask You, Lord.
    It has puzzled me often:
why do weeds grow easier than flowers?

I see it right before my eyes:
    I sow flowers and produce weeds.
    I sow grass and raise nettles;
my frail plants are choked by luscious dandelions.

Now I have no personal animosity against dandelions,
        Master.
    They are bright, jolly flowers.
    Sensible, too, for they shut up at night,
    which is more than many people do
    judging by the noise one hears.

But why should dandelions that I don't plant
    thrive better than the flowers I protect?
    How is it that from a packet of choice seeds
I raise chickweed?

If it were only a question of flowers and weeds
    it would be strange enough,
    but the tendency goes further and deeper.
    I find it within my own being,
    a downward pull,
    a gravitation to a lower level.

It is a daily fight to keep the standard high,
     to bring forth flowers instead of weeds,
     good instead of evil
     in my life, character and service.

Lord, is it a law in Your moral world,
     as well as in Your natural world,
that the more valuable the product
     the harder it is to produce?

Just a Moment, Lord

14 MARCH

A HUMAN CATERPILLAR

I'M just a caterpillar, Master, earthbound and clumsy,
     heavy feet hugging the ground;
     a crawler, eyes glued to a cabbage leaf.
     Slow, painfully slow in progress.
Limited activity, limited vision, limited horizon.

But, in my heart, my caterpillar-heart, I dream . . .
dream of the day when I shall shed my cumbrous clothing,
     say goodbye to my clodfootedness,
     rise from my chrysalis-coffin,
and on flashing wings skim the eternities of the upper sphere.

Free! free at last, free of my former fetters, denizen of another
                    world.
'This perishable thing clothed with the imperishable,
this mortal clothed with immortality.'
     O great, glad day!
     O hope within my soul,
     O glorious promise,
     destiny divine!
But just now, Lord, I'm still at the crawling stage,
     earthbound and clumsy,
     heavy feet hugging the ground, slow, painfully slow in progress.

In Your goodness grant me this favour, dear Lord;
let not my sluggish gait rob me of my vision.
     I shall rise clothed with immortality
     to join You in the Great Beyond!
It is Your own promise, Lord, and on that promise I rely.

Just a Moment, Lord

ANNABELLA JONES

LORD, what can I do about Annabella Jones?
How I feel about her can hardly have escaped Your notice,
    for she calls out the worst in me.

At sight of her I sprout prickles all over,
    feel my nerves on edge
    and my temper rising.

If You ask me to define my objections, I can't do it.
    Everything about her irritates me.
    To start with, her name!
I know she isn't responsible for what her parents called her,
but that knowledge doesn't change my feelings
    which are quite unreasonable.
No one has the right to tack a name like Annabella
    on to plain Jones.
It isn't my business, I know, Master,
    but it annoys me all the same. What can I do about it?

Lord, I come to You, all hot and bothered and unreasonable.
Calm me down, quieten me, make me sensible.
Teach me not to get upset over small matters.
Don't let a person's name come between us,
    nor the colour of her hair,
    nor the way she walks
    or how she talks.

Make me a better mixer with all kinds of people, Lord.
    Let me accept them for what they are,
    try to find their good points
    and overlook the rest.

Just a Moment, Lord

MINOR IRRITATIONS

SMALL irritations have a way of growing into great mountains. We all have our own ways, of course, but unfortunately ours always seem right and other people's wrong! The husband, orderly in everything, squeezes the toothpaste from the bottom of the tube, folding it up as it is used, and replacing the cap each time.

The wife, living life more lightly, squeezes happily from the middle of the tube, leaving it bent and capless. There are words, recriminations, quarrels and the scene is set for a future divorce.

The obvious solution is to have two individual tubes of toothpaste, but our young couple are too hot-headed to think of that.

When two people live closely one to another, someone has to give way for the sake of peace. But it should never be the same person all the time. Personal tastes must be respected. I have read that they are inherited, so there is not much that one can do about it. One must not try to force or tease another to eat what is unpleasant to them.

Hints for Living

MY HEART SINGS

TODAY my heart sings, Lord;
Everything within me rejoices.

> Joy bubbles up in my soul,
> overflows and cascades like a stream
> leaping all barriers;
> the joy of knowing You,
> the joy of union with You.

One with You, Creator of the world,
and my Creator,
one with You, Saviour of the world,
and my Saviour.
One with You, Spirit of the eternal God,
and my God,
one with You, almighty King of kings
and my Lord and King.

> Joy, joy at the heart of living,
> joy in doing, joy in being;
> sing for joy, my heart,
> for sheer joy, my soul.

> The joy of loving You,
> the joy of following You,
> the joy of serving You;
> all the way 'long it is glory.

Today my heart sings, Lord;
everything within me rejoices,
joy bubbles up in my soul,
glory . . . glory!

Just a Moment, Lord

HAVES AND HAVE-NOTS

MASTER, the world seems to be divided
    between the haves and the have-nots.
Politicians say: 'Let us take from those who have
    and give to those who have not, then all will be equal.'
It sounds feasible and indeed reasonable,
    especially from the standpoint of the have-nots.

Your words, Lord, were quite different.
You said: 'To him that has shall be given,
    and from him that has not
    shall be taken the little he has.'
It's very baffling to reflect upon Your teaching.

I think I see a glimmer of light, Lord,
    and You must help me to more clarity.
Politicians are talking about material benefits
    but You were speaking of spiritual values
    of infinite and eternal worth.
It is the little grain of faith that releases
    the floodtide of Your response,
the tiny effort of following You
    which calls forth Your companionship,
the time given to prayer which facilitates Your access,
the willingness to listen to Your voice that brings guidance.

I see it, Lord.
Those who make no spiritual effort remain outside, untouched.
The trembling radiance of a divine world surrounds them
    but cannot reach them
for they have shut the door and darkened the windows.

Thank You, Lord, for the little I do know of You.
Increase it mightily, I pray.

Between You and Me, Lord

USE IT OR . . .

AN American doctor has launched a USE IT OR LOSE IT! campaign in the interests of health. His thesis is that any faculty of mind or body that falls into disuse will soon be lost for ever. We all know how little-used muscles complain when we tackle a gardening job or a special clean-up round the house. Those who have not cycled for years will find their leg muscles in very poor trim, and swimmers know that constant practice is necessary to maintain form. Many of us who have struggled for years to learn a foreign language know to our cost how rapidly our former fluency can deteriorate.

I am sure the soul's functions are affected by the same law. A period of prayerlessness makes prayer all the harder when we are driven by our need to seek the Lord again. Let us strive to keep our mental, physical and spiritual powers at their best by constant, applied use.

Along the Way

USE OR LOSE

MASTER, I always imagine You and Your disciples
walking leisurely along the roads of Palestine,
talking earnestly in small groups.
     You never caught a bus or train
and I never think of You running or jogging,
     yet I remind myself
that You often climbed into the hills
and that must have been strenuous.

Our lives are much more sedentary, Lord,
and we must make an effort to get exercise.
Given muscles, we must use them or lose their elasticity;
given minds, we must stretch them by reading,
     learning and thinking
or we shall slow down mentally;
given an eternal soul we must nourish it,
     use its powers, develop it continually,
and that we can only do under Your tuition, Lord.

The sportsman has to practise to maintain form,
the pianist to keep his fingers flexible,
the dancer to improve body control,
the linguist to retain his knowledge . . .
Then how can we expect to learn
     the way of prayer
     unless we persevere in praying?
A period of prayerlessness makes praying harder.
Help me to make it a daily habit
     whether I feel like it or not.
So will my spiritual senses be kept alive
     and I shall remain in contact with You, Master.

My God and I

21 March

A BIT OF MY MIND

I GAVE her a bit of my mind, Master!
  I spoke out
   hot and sharp.
I told her what I thought.
She had touched me on the raw and
   she got her desserts . . .
I could argue so with good reason
but inside, in my better self,
   I felt ashamed.

The bit of my mind that I gave her
   was the worst bit,
the part I would rather not possess,
the scratchy, resentful, touchy self
that I would gladly get rid of if I could.
It surfaces during moments of stress
   when I am tired,
   overburdened, depressed
   or just plain awkward.
If I can never be quit of it
at least I should like to curb it better,
   keep it in check,
   hold it on a tight leash,
so that in a flare-up of momentary anger
   it cannot slip its restraints
   and wound another person.
I need Your assistance, Lord, in this matter.
   Please help me!

My God and I

22 March

COILS OF SIN

WHAT a coil of sin the human heart contains!

Someone has said that it is like an onion. Peel off one layer and there lies another beneath.

But how great is God's mercy! In spite of our meanness, our littleness, our smouldering resentments and blazing hates he loves us, he accepts us. In order to change us he has forgiven us with a boundless love.

Ur Minnets Gömmor (Down Memory Lane)

NEITHER WORSE NOR BETTER

IT has been said that when we get older, we become neither worse nor better, but only more like ourselves. That is one more reason for wanting to be the sort of person we should like to have as a friend.

Hints for Living

SPRING CLEANING

HONESTLY, Master, I didn't know the paintwork was so dirty!
That dust not only settles but bites itself fast,
    experience has taught me.
It was a revelation what a good wash-over would do,
not only cleaning it but making it reflect light
    so that the whole area glowed
and my heart glowed with satisfaction too.

It was the sun that started it. Your sun, Lord.
My inward cheer when it broke through the clouds
    after days of gloom was followed by a moment of truth
when I saw what the light revealed.
During the dull winter months the room looked quite clean
but under the sun's revealing eye it looked grubby.
I could hardly believe my eyes when I saw a cobweb
    in the corner of the ceiling.
To my knowledge no spider lives in this house, yet there it was,
    evidence of an unseen sharer of my abode.
I hastened to rob my invisible lodger of his airy hammock
    as a delicate hint that he should change his quarters.

One truth I learnt, Lord,
is that partial cleaning is worse than no cleaning,
    worse at least in that it shows.
One polished window shows up the grimy ones;
    having begun one has to finish.

My thoughts moved along that thread,
    drawing it out to spiritual dimensions.
A word from Your Book came to my mind with
    singular comfort:
'He who has begun a good work in you will continue it.'
I'm trusting You to do just that, Lord.
Go on working in my heart and life,
preparing me for the day when I shall be with You.

Between You and Me, Lord

GOD-FLIGHT

LORD, this instinct to avoid You,
　　　to hide away,
　　　seems universal,
but why should I seek to escape from You?
Is it because I fear You,
　　　or feel guilty
　　　or unworthy?

Where shall I hide when You are everywhere?
The top of Everest is as accessible to You
　　　as the deepest mine shaft.
The blare of my radio or TV can't drown
　　　Your voice within.
Locked doors and curtained windows do not keep You out.
　　　Where can one hide?

The answer is *nowhere*!
Flight is not the solution to the problem.
　　　The true response is surrender.
God is not after me to punish me
　　　but to win me,
not to blame me but forgive me.
Why then should I seek to hide?

O God, take this fear of You from my heart . . .
Let me look up into Your face and say:
　　　Here I am, Lord,
　　　You've won!

God in My Everyday

WEDDING DAY

I'M excited and yet afraid, Lord.
Now my wedding day has dawned I hesitate
　　　and tremble . . .
It is such a momentous step to take
　　　into a mysterious veiled future.
Even now as I talk to You, Master,
the threads of the day's events are twining together
　　　in a pre-arranged pattern
to culminate in the high spot of the ceremony.

Before I pledge myself to my husband,
I want to give myself once more to You.
I invite You, Lord, to be the first guest
in our new home:
invisible yet potently present,
influencing all we say and do,
guiding us in all our decisions.

I'm so glad that You chose to be present
at the wedding in Cana of Galilee
in Your days on earth, Master,
for it shows that You can share the highest joys,
the fun and laughter,
bringing them a new element of happiness.
I might otherwise have thought of You too often
as the Man of Sorrows
and left You out of my planning
for supreme moments of bliss.

Join with us, Lord, as we make our solemn vows,
and remain with us in the family fun that will follow.
May this be a day which we shall both remember
as the happiest day of our life.
With Your blessing, it can be so.

Towards You, Lord

27 MARCH

DEVELOP YOURSELF

ONE of the most comforting facts in life is that we are living material. We have not been poured out in a mould, left to set and to live like that to the end of our days. We each have to work at ourselves as long as life shall last.

We can work at ourselves to get rid of our awkward corners (and we all have some) and to increase inward harmony. It can be fun to try to work against our failings, to produce flowers where before there have been weeds in our character.

God does not want us to be robots, machines programmed to do right always. He has given us free will so that we can choose to do good or evil, but he stands ready to come to our aid when we ask him to help us. It is in God's plan that we should grow in grace and in the knowledge of our Lord and Saviour, Jesus Christ, but without that power of choice there could be no growth.

Hints for Living

EVERYTHING NEW

IT'S a thrill, Master, all this newness around me.
New clothes, new furniture, new carpets.
I could dance around my little home in happiness.
And yet I am afraid . . .
afraid of spoiling all this pristine cleanness,
afraid of using the oven in case I stain it,
afraid of spilling on the gleaming carpet,
afraid of chipping one of the best cups.

Why should I feel afraid like this, Master?
Alas, I know the answer.

All my life I have been painfully aware
that freshness wears off.
That the simple fact of being used wears the surface away,
gives things an older look.
Each time I have worn a new dress or shoes or coat,
I have determined to keep them like new
but it has been impossible.
Wear and tear show in some way.

I remind myself, though, that antiques command higher
prices
than newly acquired goods.
Perhaps I need that philosophy, Master,
to use with care
so that these our possessions age gracefully.
I pray that for myself as well, Lord.
I too cannot escape the marks of living,
for in some way it will show
however hard I try to keep the wrinkles at bay.
Help me to mature with grace.

One thing I would ask, Master.
Let our new-found union, so filled with joy,
never become casual and perfunctory.
Let it be refreshed and renewed day by day,
through the joy of Your presence in our lives.

Towards You, Lord

AFTERMATH

WHAT a rush life can be, Lord!
I feel worn out with work and home duties
        exhausting my strength
        and straining my nerves.
I have been a bit bad-tempered lately, I admit,
        but that is because of stress.
I thought married life would be easier
        and I find it has its pitfalls.

Just the sharing of cupboards can be traumatic.
A woman needs a lot of room for her clothes,
        an extra share of wardrobe space,
        but somehow he can't see that, Master.
Then meals . . . he likes a hearty breakfast
        and I am permanently slimming.
He likes coffee, I prefer tea, but it is a bother to make both.
Why should I always have to give in to him?
Can people so different in their ways
        learn to live in harmony,
without one capitulating to the other?

I love, admire and respect my husband
        but we are *two people,* Lord!
When we united our lives,
        we didn't merge our personalities.
        I'm still me!
Help me, Lord, in this matter.
I want my marriage to succeed and last.
Help us both to seek a peaceful compromise
        when opinions differ,
and let us work to achieve harmony between ourselves
and within the walls we are proud to call our home.

Towards You, Lord

IMPROVEMENT POSSIBLE

THERE is always some improvement possible as we work towards the possession of a harmonious personality. It is interesting to ask ourselves *why* we did this and that, and thus find out something of the motives behind our action.

Hints for Living

ABOUT MRS FELL

I'D like to talk to You about Mrs Fell, Lord.
To say that she and I are not on the same wavelength
      is putting it too mildly;
We are directly antagonistic and for no known reason.
She is a most excellent woman.
The perfect wife mentioned in Your Book couldn't hold
      a candle to her;
      yet while I admire her
      I dislike her.
Am I simply jealous of her
      because her virtues show up my shortcomings?

I want to love Mrs Fell.
No! that's not exactly the truth, Master.
I *don't* want to love Mrs Fell!
Very definitely not.
I must put my desire in another form:
I want You to make me love her.
No! that's not true either.
I must find another formula.

I'd like You to take from me that which makes me dislike
      her.
(I'd like You to do a bit of work on her too,
      for I'm sure she heartily dislikes me.)
But if You would just show me where the fault lies in me,
that would be the beginning of a new approach;
and a new approach might lead to better understanding,
and better understanding to mutual regard.

I'm sorry to give You all this trouble, Lord.
I ought to have brought this matter to You long ago.
      Forgive my tardiness.
In Your goodness help me to get straight on this point,
then there will be one less problem in my life.

Just a Moment, Lord

A DUNCE IN YOUR SCHOOL

LORD, I've muffed it again!
I'm just a dunce in Your school.
      I knew I had failed,
      and You knew it too,
      but You said nothing.
Have patience with me!
I'm always going over the same old lessons
and never really learning them.

I was so sure I could handle that situation.
      I've had plenty of experience of it
      and through trial and error have learnt what not to do,
      so I had the theory all right.

I'm sure that if You tested me in theory only
      I could make a better showing.
      But You are not satisfied with theory.
      You insist upon practice,
      and that is where I fail.
Why, Lord, should there be such a gulf fixed
      between theory and practice?
      To know what to do
      and yet not do it;
      to see the pitfalls
      and yet stumble into them?

Do You tire of having such a poor pupil, and
feel like washing Your hands of me?
      Give me another chance!
Perhaps You can show me a better way to learn my lessons,
      so that I don't fail so often.
I want to learn, I really do.
I'm beginning to see that the secret is
      to keep in close touch with You,
      rather than to rely on theoretical knowledge
      or my own endeavours.

Teach me then, Master, so that I can make some progress;
I don't want to stay for ever the dunce in Your school.

Just a Moment, Lord

A SIMPLE SUM

THAT was a simple sum You set Peter, Master.
       Seventy times seven . . .
Any child could give the answer:
       four hundred and ninety.
But to forgive a man four hundred and ninety times
       is a hard task;
       infinitely hard.
It goes against the grain,
like so many other of Your commands.

What that person did against me was not so serious,
       but it stung my pride,
       it wounded my self-esteem.
If I've forgiven her once, I've forgiven her a dozen times,
       for there's the rub, Master!

It's not four hundred and ninety separate faults that I
       need Your help to forgive,
I have to keep on forgiving her for the same old fault,
       way back in the past, done with long ago.
       I'm ashamed to own it, Lord,
       but You know it's true,
       so why should I try to hide it?

Even when I want to forgive, my forgiveness is not complete.
       Deep down within me a memory lies buried.
       Association wakes it to life;
       the reawakening brings fresh resentment;
       and I have to seek Your grace to forgive again.

O Master, if You treated me like that,
       where should I be?
You forgive and forget once and for all.
My sins are sunk in the bottomless sea of Your mercy and love.
Dig deep, Lord, deep into the depths of my heart,
Down where these old sores lie festering.
       Pour in Your healing love,
       teach me to forgive
       as You forgive me,
       once and for all.

Just a Moment, Lord

DOUBLE VISION

WE know very well that if we see double we need to visit the oculist and have our eyes tested. But at times double vision is caused by outward circumstances.

Long ago when, as a young Salvation Army Captain, I started to work at our Paris headquarters, it was the custom at midday to take lunch down in the basement dining-room. I was assigned a place at a table for four. Being new and nervous I hardly dared to raise my eyes from my plate, but I was conscious of being in the centre of quite a large room with rows of small tables at each side of me. I felt quite overwhelmed to be in the centre of such a large group of officers and employees.

It was not until several days later that I really looked around me and found out that at my right side was a large mirror stretching the whole surface of the wall. What I had taken to be many more people at my right was simply the reflection of those on my left. To my great surprise the dining room was really quite small!

In some ways that experience is a parable of life. Many situations which overwhelm us and frighten us are not so important in themselves. It is what we think about them which makes them appear so threatening. We must have the courage really to look our problems and anxieties in the face. Many of them will then shrink in size.

Ur Minnets Gömmor (Down Memory Lane)

DISTORTED VISION

ANOTHER strange effect caused by a mirror, I noticed in a lift in a building which we have sometimes visited in Uleåborg, in Finland.

The mirror is bevelled in such a way that one sees oneself in many different sizes, each smaller than the previous one. Instead of there being one of you there are 20 or more. You fill the world, at least the world of the lift you are in.

That, too, is a parable of life.

Some people think the world revolves round themselves. In every problem, every possibility, they see only themselves and how it will affect them in the present or in the future.

The two mirrors I have described teach me that I must take a middle way. My world must not be filled with other people to the extent that I am tense and frightened. Nor must it be filled only with myself and my own interests. There is a middle line which I must seek to follow by God's help.

Ur Minnets Gömmor (Down Memory Lane)

A DISTORTED PICTURE

YOU must forgive us, Master.
We mean well when we talk so much of Your love
  and soft-pedal Your anger;
but we are giving a distorted picture,
  a wrong image, a one-sided view of You.

We avoid the issue by omitting to read
  Your scornful words on subterfuge,
  Your hatred of hypocrisy,
  Your blazing anger against injustices,
  Your sharp words to tricksters.
You lashed out against the religious humbugs of Your day;
  'play actors' You called them,
  'hypocrites' You hurled at them,
  'blind leaders of the blind',
  'brood of vipers'.
  You did not spare hard words.

You couldn't expect to be popular when You used such language.
  You cut across vested interests,
  You stirred up hatred,
  You created enemies,
  and You paid the penalty with Your life.
Help us, Lord, to remember Your anger against deceit.
  Don't let us imagine we can double-cross You,
  pretending to be what we are not,
  or think that we can sow without reaping.

Lord, You are flaming justice as well as tender love;
give us a wholesome fear of Your condemnation.

Just a Moment, Lord

THE NEW DRESS

THOUGH hardly successful at home dressmaking, from time to time I yield to temptation. So there was I with a length of delightful blue stuff, silkily soft to the touch and unobtrusively adorned with tiny flowers.

To make sure of success I bought a new pattern. Cutting out required a good deal of courage, but finally all was ready for sewing. Then I found an unexpected snag – the material kept slipping. A friend kindly told me I needed a special kind of needle in my machine. With that I made better progress, but the intricacy of the design baffled me so that I had to tack, sew, take to pieces, retack and resew, several times over. By the time I finished, I was sick of the sight of it! I knew I could never wear it but a solution occurred to me. I offered the dress to my daughter. She took one look and sniffed. 'No one under 40 would be seen wearing a thing like that,' she affirmed.

Next I tried my granddaughter of 16. She was enraptured! She accepted it with delight on the spot and wore it for special occasions and parties. She looked entrancing in it . . . The moral – if there is a moral – is that one person's cast-off is another's lucky find.

Along the Way

7 April

HEAVEN MUST BE VAST

HEAVEN must be a vast place, Lord!
Myriads of souls from all corners of the earth
　　　　made welcome by Your love
　　　　for them as individuals.
It is beyond all human imagination . . .
Mrs Jones and Mrs Smith who attend the same church
　　　　but never speak to each other
　　　　will not easily be placed.
Their husbands, long-time rivals,
are also likely to make sparks fly,
adding to the display of shooting stars.

Have You some sphere, Lord,
perhaps one of Your 'black holes' in space
where such contrary characters – millions of them –
　　　　can cool off through the ages
　　　　until they learn more sense?

Will theological controversy cease
　　　　as we pass the Heavenly threshold,
or shall we require barriers between the sects
　　　　to keep the peace?
Shall we challenge Peter and Paul on aspects
　　　　of their letters in Your Book,
or listen to lectures as they defend their standpoints?
It is hopeless, Lord, to imagine Your Heavenly realm.
　　　　Forgive our human inability
　　　　to comprehend Your master-mind.
You will find a way to accommodate us all
in the vast Heaven prepared for Your children.

God in My Everyday

THE GARLANDED CROSS (GOOD FRIDAY)

THE wayside crucifix stood high, its foot
    deeply planted among heavy stones.
I had to raise my head to glimpse
the twisted features of the suffering Christ.
    The sculptor had been lavish
in his portrayal of blood from wounds
    in hands, feet and side.
I stood in silence, remembering, worshipping,
    before I turned away.

A coach load of tourists passed me
    in hilarious mood, singing and shouting.
A mocking cheer greeted the crucified Christ.
From the open windows some threw paper streamers
    at the figure on the cross,
garlanding it with multi-coloured bands
which fluttered in the breeze.
    Someone protested angrily
and the driver drew up to allow a man to descend.
He tried to climb the cross but it was too high,
so he had to leave the wind to strip it
    of its gaudy trimmings.

With revulsion in my heart, Lord,
    I tried to pray,
but all I could say was the echo
    of Your words, Master, from Calvary:
'Father, forgive them, for they know not what they do.'

God in My Everyday

RUNAWAY HORSES

CERTAIN moments leave an indelible impression as though a mental camera takes an instantaneous picture which remains sharply etched in the memory. One such picture remains with me from Santiago, Chile.

I had just closed the front door behind me when I heard screams and the hard galloping of horses' hooves. Looking down the street I saw a dustman's cart in wild career drawn by its two powerful horses, their manes flying in the wind, their teeth bared in fright. Women shrieked and pressed themselves against the walls of the houses as the cart rocked from side to side of the street, sometimes mounting the pavement.

Suddenly there was a loud crash, a wild pawing of hooves, then silence. The runaways had met a car head on and been severely injured. A couple of bullets soon put them out of their misery.

I am reminded of this incident when young people today insist on having their freedom. Those two horses had their freedom for a few hectic minutes. No reins held them in. Nothing restrained them.

One can understand youth longing to be free of all restraint. We who are old have known that feeling, but there was less opportunity in our youth for us to express ourselves and find our own way. For that very reason we were saved from many catastrophes which might have overtaken us.

We were curbed too severely. Now we must find a new way with youth, freedom coupled with responsibility; freedom under a certain restraint, accepted willingly as the rules of the game of life.

Ur Minnets Gömmor (Down Memory Lane)

MY LIVING LORD (EASTER)

MASTER, I believe in Your resurrection!
You are my living Lord!
My mind tries to recapture the scene . . .

Slow dawning . . .
with the chill of night still present.
Shrouded forms of women steal silently along, going where?
To the tomb . . . to weep.
Heavy their hearts, laboured their breathing,
slow their steps.

Daylight!
A clutch of fear at their hearts,
a gasp of awe
at the stone back-rolled,
the tomb empty!

O panting hesitation . . .
O growing expectation . . .
a glimpse, a shout, a stab of joy.
'He is not here. He is risen!'
Waves of ecstasy.
It is as He said:
He is not dead but risen.
Alive! My Lord is alive!

God in My Everyday

THE GREAT BEYOND

I WISH You had told us more about the Great Beyond, Lord.
    We're all heading there whether we like it or not.
    By air, rail, road, sea, or on plain Shanks's pony,
    we're all on our way into the Unknown.
It's not easy for our western minds to understand You
    when You talk in picture language.
    You must forgive our denseness
        and our terrible literal-mindedness.

Your servant Paul told of being snatched up to the third heaven.
    Was that just a phrase he used to indicate highest bliss,
        as we speak today of being in the seventh heaven?
    Or are there really stages in the Beyond?
Is the third heaven the tourist class, so to speak,
    with possibility of rising to first class?
    Or is the third heaven the utmost pinnacle of joy?
To be quite frank with You, Master,
    I feel a bit scared at times.
        Not of You, but of the Unknown.

I am comforted when I think of the repentant thief,
    dying on the cross next to Yours.
When he turned to You in his utter need,
You promised that he should be with You in Paradise.
Where is Paradise? What is Paradise?
    Is it the forecourt of Heaven,
    or Heaven itself?
I don't know. But the operative thought is 'with You'.
    So when I feel afraid, I comfort myself . . . I shall be with You
        and all will be well.

Just a Moment, Lord

THE WINDOW SILL OF HEAVEN

OPEN your hearts to receive these words of William Blake:
    Every morning lean thine arms
    Upon the window sill of Heaven
    And gaze upon thy Lord;
    Then with the vision in thy heart
    Turn, strong to meet thy day.

Why can't we all pass on helpful thoughts to each other both by letter and by speech? Such thoughts last longer than a bunch of flowers and can bring refreshment to our minds even during the night when we lie awake.

Let's be more generous in this way!

Along the Way

A REBUKE

LORD, I have received a rebuke.
Not from You, Master, although I might well deserve it.
      But from a young man.
He said nothing to me; he did nothing to me;
      but I saw him,
      and seeing, I was humbled and contrite.

He sat in a restaurant, his plate before him.
He ate like a dog, Master, just like a dog.
Lapping up ice-cream with his lips and tongue
      direct from the plate.

My inward reaction was swift . . . and unforgivable.
      Modern youth!
      What new monstrosity will they invent?
And then I watched and understood.

His twisted arms hung uselessly on his knees.
He was a cripple, a young cripple;
      going through life with a terrible defect.

And in my heart I had blamed him,
blamed him for unseemly behaviour, this fine,
      brave lad,
suffering people's pitying gaze each day of his life;
      living differently because he must;
      each day a new crucifixion.
Forgive me, Master.
I take this rebuke as from You.

Help me not to judge without knowing,
      not to jump to conclusions,
      not to condemn without evidence,
      nor to hurt any of my fellow men needlessly,
      remembering that to know all is to forgive all.

Just a Moment, Lord

SOUL AND BODY

LORD, what a strange double nature I have!
Am I a body hosting a soul
     as an honoured guest,
or a soul imprisoned in a body
     and longing for freedom?
Part of myself – my body – is perishable
     yet it is the part I know best;
the only part of me that I can see and recognise as myself.

That shadowy thing within me –
     call it soul or spirit –
is the undying part that will live on
     beyond the grave, *the real me* . . .
yet I hardly know it, Lord.

     It is Your law, Master,
that soul shall be housed in body throughout life.
Not like a kernel in a nutshell, loosely rolling round,
but joined by many invisible bonds,
interacting the one upon the other.
I can starve my soul while feeding my body
or enrich my soul while denying my body.
Help me to strike a right balance, Master, so that both
     can enjoy Your blessing;
the good health of the body
     becoming a potent vehicle for the soul,
the soul's harmony spilling peace into the nerves
and muscles as long as life shall last.

God in My Everyday

THE LAWN

THANK You, Lord, for the greenness of growing things,
for the cheery patch of freshness that is my lawn.
     Not perfect, oh no!
Marred by weeds, starred by daisies, but green, how green!
As I stood and looked at it I heard Your voice, Master,
     pointing a spiritual lesson.
I was in the right mood to receive it.
Each tiny plant or grass is green, You said,
     because it has an individual root.

No blade is held up by its neighbours,
supported by their communal strength;
it must draw its own nourishment from the soil.
No chance for laziness there!
No relying on others
and being carried along by the crowd.
Each must seek its food from the soil and air
or else a dead patch results.

You used the opportunity well, Master,
to remind me that spiritual life is very personal.

Massed in Your living church Your children present a bold front,
a mighty array,
but only as each one is alive in You individually
can they remain a force for good.

Keep me alive, Lord! Part of the whole, yes,
but also alive if I have to stand alone and witness for You.
Let green shoots of growing be seen in my spiritual life,
let my soul flourish,
because its roots draw strength from Your hidden supplies.

Between You and Me, Lord

THE LIZARD'S TAIL

I ONCE read that if you catch a lizard by its tail, it will shed it and grow another. I regarded that as rather a 'tall' story, but seeing a lizard sunning itself in the south of France tempted me to test the statement.

Each time I stretched out my hand, the lizard opened one eye, then scuttled away. At last I managed to touch it. Instantly its tail fell off and the rest of the lizard made for safety under a ledge of rock. Fifteen minutes elapsed before all movement ceased in the tail, and only then did I leave the spot after burying the 'remains'. It was true. What sounded impossible had been proved true. With my own eyes I had seen it.

It is a long hop from a lizard's tail to salvation through Jesus Christ, yet there is a connection. Salvation from sin sounds incredible. A new spiritual life does not seem to fit in with our everyday life. So many people have said to me: 'I don't believe that God can save me.'

Sometimes we must make the experiment ourselves before we can believe. The seemingly impossible can happen. It has happened to thousands.

Be courageous and make the experiment for yourself.

Ur Minnets Gömmor (Down Memory Lane)

THE WEAVER

TODAY, Lord, I see You as the divine Weaver.
I can't believe that in the long ago
      You wound up a clockwork world
      and that You now sit back
      idly clasping Your hands as You watch it tick,
      letting it run out its time.

I see You at a living loom of myriad colours,
all lives as threads passing through Your hands.
      The ultimate pattern only You know
but Your plans are constantly hampered
      by too little human co-operation,
      by too many human mistakes
      and sins, Lord . . . black, black sins,
      making ugly patches in Your tapestry.

You would weave a future where justice and truth reign
but men's wickedness spoils Your aims,
      the perfect design cannot be.
Coarse black threads of spiritual rebellion,
      awkward knots of disobedience,
      roughen the texture of Your work,
yet intertwined among the grosser fibres
      are woven golden threads of Your love and mercy.

O patient Weaver! Never give up Your task!
No other hands can fashion good out of evil,
      beauty and joy out of life's roughage.
Take the threads of my life, imperfect as they are,
and make them part of a glorious whole.

Between You and Me, Lord

ADAPT YOURSELF (1)

WE must try to improve along the lines of our natural gifts, not dream vainly of what can never be ours. If we have no ear for music it is best not to dream of being an opera singer! We might, however, succeed in embroidery or art. If we have no voice for solo-singing, we may be able to develop as speakers or in drama. If too shy to speak in public we may be able to write. Everyone has something in which they can excel.

Hints for Living

ADAPT YOURSELF (2)

BECAUSE one door in life is closed to us we must not consider ourselves as of less worth than other people. There are other things that we can do, other arts in which we can shine, not only for the inward satisfaction it brings us but also for the pleasure it gives to others.

Hints for Living

KIND TO THE UNTHANKFUL

LORD, Your Book says that You are kind to
      the unthankful.
    I'm not like that, Master.
    I'm kind until people prove unthankful,
    and then I feel like leaving them to it,
    washing my hands of them.

But You go on being kind,
    even against anger and hate,
    scorn and cold indifference,
    wooing with love the hardened hearts of men.

Why do You do it, Lord?
Do You spy the glint of gold among the rubble?
Can You see the makings of a man in a ne'er-do-well?
Or sense the texture of fine womanhood in a slut?
Or can You do it just because You are You?
    Because You really do care about people,
    really love them in spite of their nastiness?

I think that must be the secret,
    and that is why I react differently.
You pour out love in such abundance
    that it sweeps around and over all obstacles.
You love because it is Your nature to love,
    without thought of recompense or return.
Is love like that something one can learn, Master?
    Or has it to be a gift,
    a gift from You?
    If so, will You grant it me,
    in the measure that I can contain it?

Just a Moment, Lord

ADOPTED

MOST children go through that phase.
    I remember it clearly, Lord.
Brooding by myself over some rebuke
    for bad behaviour,
I decided that seeing my parents had such
    different ideas from mine,
I could not be their child. I must be adopted!
Then my imagination took over and for many days
    with secret enjoyment
I built up the scenario.
My real parents were from high society,
    possibly even royal.

I had been snatched from my pram despite
    my nurse's brave resistance.
Later I had been abandoned when the ransom
    was not paid.

Master, as I look back at the many fanciful patterns
    I wove on that theme,
I wonder at their ingenuity.
Finally I accepted that I really belonged
    to Mum and Dad,
aware that facial likeness supported that theory!

Later I learned that I really had been adopted,
    not by my parents
    but by *You*, Master!
Adopted into the family of God,
truly belonging there through Your grace and mercy.
How can I ever thank You enough?

My God and I

SOMEONE'S PET CORN

TODAY I trod on someone's pet corn, Master,
hard, ruthlessly but unintentionally.
How was I to know, Lord, that just that subject was his
    sore point?
    I had never seen the man before.

Why should a few innocent remarks awake such anger?
I tried to think of the soft answer that might turn away his wrath,
but, Lord, You know I am not nimble-witted in such matters.
The gracious and disarming reply does not rise naturally
                          and quickly within me.
So I bowed my head and let the storm pass over.
        I felt sorry afterward, Lord, for he was worried,
        tense, overburdened, nervy and explosive,
        ready-laid kindling for any stray spark.
And I struck the match which made him flare.

Somewhere there must have been a fire extinguisher,
but my eyes couldn't see it, my hands couldn't grasp it.
Perhaps I really didn't look for it hard enough . . .
        and the mischief was done.

I'm sorry, Lord.
        Sorry for that servant of Yours whose nerves were on edge.
        Sorry that I was the stumbling-block over which he tripped.
Please, dear Lord, would You bless him just now.
Let him forget this incident, as I will try to forget it.
Make us both just a little wiser next time we meet,
                and let us meet as friends.

Just a Moment, Lord

23 APRIL

UNDERSTAND YOURSELF

SOMETIMES we do and say things which we afterwards regret and we say:
'Whatever made me do that?' Everyone is conscious of the fact that he/she
has better or worse days. Some scientists claim to have found three rhythms
of behaviour which influence us all – the physical cycle lasting 23 days
which affects our endurance; the emotional lasting 28 days which affects our
creative ideas and optimism, and the intellectual rhythm lasting 33 days,
controlling memory and clarity of thinking.

You can imagine how one feels when one is down on all three circles at
one and the same time! Scientists claim it is at such times that accidents
happen at work, children get bad reports in school and married couples
decide that they should seek a divorce.

It is most necessary, then, not to take any decisive step when we feel
'under the weather'. Wait a few days for feelings to improve and we shall see
that the situation is not as bad as we had imagined. It is a good rule 'never
to get out of the train in the tunnel!' Wait until you come out into the light
so that you can see and judge events more truly.

Hints for Living

PRAYING AWAY LOCUSTS

FEW of us know anything of the disaster which a plague of locusts can bring. In the Argentine my father once helped to fight against a locust army creeping along the ground. A broad belt of grass was fired. Inside that a trench was dug and filled with water. The insects simply walked into the fire in their thousands, their oily bodies causing dense smoke to rise. Thousands upon thousands followed until their very numbers put out the fire. The next hazard, the watery ditch, was conquered in the same manner. The first thousands of locusts drowned and filled the ditch, then the others crawled over their dead bodies. My father and others rode horses back and forward across the path of the insects, the horses dragging branches of trees behind them to sweep away the insects.

It was all to no avail.

Next morning the farmlands could not show one single green blade or leaf. The locusts had even entered the house and eaten up the sheets from the bed and the curtains at the windows. So it is easily understood that a swarm of locusts is feared, and all means are taken to divert the path of the insect hordes as they swarm and advance.

Once on holiday in the Argentine we were staying on a large sheep farm. As we walked through the fields one day, the tall grasses reaching nearly to our shoulders, hundreds of small locusts filled the air with their buzzing sound. Our hostess turned to me and said: 'Last year we had a bad time with the locusts. Now I believe that if we do something for God he will do something for us, and I want you to pray that we shall be spared such losses from locusts this year.'

That posed more than one problem for me. To start with, I do not believe that God 'rewards' us by doing something for us, just because we try to do something for him.

Secondly, is the desire to escape from the usual hazards of living and working a legitimate subject of prayer for a Christian?

I tried to answer tactfully, saying that God gives us far more than we deserve in his daily mercies and his unending love, but that I could not undertake to pray away locusts from her crops.

What would you have said?

Ur Minnets Gömmor (Down Memory Lane)

CHANGING MOODS

ALL God's children can speak of times of dryness as well as joy, of periods of darkness as well as light, of valley experiences as well as moments on the mountain top with our Lord. We should do well to realise that these changing moods are part of the natural rhythm, and that the fact that we do not feel God to be near does not mean that he is afar off. We must learn to walk by faith.

Hints for Living

HALF-TRUTHS

HOW do You regard half-truths, Master?
In Your reckoning do two half-truths equal a whole truth,
      or do they add up to one big, whopping lie?
      I hope the former,
      but I fear the latter;
      and my fear is greater than my hope.
Can truth be halved or quartered?
Can it be coloured, shaded or distorted?
      Or is it immutable, inviolable?

Your Book reminds me that You are truth,
      and that knowledge makes me wary of You,
      for You know all.
In Your presence my cleverest subtleties fail to register,
      my rationalisations are transparent,
      my self-deceptions dissolve;
and I stand revealed, unprotected, in the blazing light
      of Your absolute truth.

Lord, is it possible for me to be completely truthful,
to balance my words on the hair-spring of absolute truth,
to think without my thought being tinted by my fears or desires,
not to deviate from the plumb line of truth
      by a glance,
      a tone of voice,
      a shrug of the shoulders,
      a calculated emphasis.
      a nod of approval,
      a sniff of disdain,
      a lengthened pause . . . ?

Master, grant me sincerity! Make me truthful.
Let Your light search me as I can bear it,
      and so prepare me for the day
      when I shall be exposed to all its intensity.

Just a Moment, Lord

BETWEEN YOU AND ME

I SEE it clearly, Lord.
Every single thing that happens
   is ultimately between You and me,
   just the two of us alone.
No matter who is sitting beside me,
no matter how many people crowd around
   or whether I am at home or abroad,
in the final analysis it is my relationship to You that counts.

There is the outside me that other people know:
   how I walk and talk,
   how I dress and eat,
   what I like and dislike.
Folk could write an essay on all that
and yet I should find it difficult to accept
   for it wouldn't be the *real* me.

The real me only You know fully.
The inner person that only partially expresses itself,
   that struggles for life
against the bonds of the body encumbering it,
that flutters and strains for it hardly knows what,
striving for something greater than it can express . . .
This hidden self You know and understand,
and I am glad in that knowledge.

That is why all that happens is finally
   just between You and me,
for You are the only one who can truly judge me.
You are reality, the unchangeable truth,
and a spark of Your eternal spirit has been lit in my heart
   drawing me to You,
   linking me with You,
   invisibly and eternally.

Between You and Me, Lord

NO SECRETS

THERE can be no secrets between You and me, Master,
   and I am glad about that.
I can carry off a camouflage with other people.
A sudden shopping emergency sees me sally forth,

a neat coat hiding my worn overall
with its newly acquired spots of paint
          (I do slosh it around rather generously).
I wouldn't like Mrs Black to know what my coat hides,
for she would gloat for ages over my slovenliness.

Then I can control my impatience with certain people
          up to a point,
          for rather a limited space of time, I admit.
I kid myself that I am getting through nicely
but You know quite well how I am boiling inside.
You see the rising resentment that my time is being abused,
          the growing irritation
          while my face still wears – at least I hope it does –
          a sympathetic smile.
You hold Your peace but I seem to catch
          a reproachful look.

Lord, I can't wear my heart on my sleeve.
I must hide some of my feelings from curious gazes.
Sometimes I have to suppress a bitter disappointment,
trying not to reveal how wounded I am.
It is such a relief then, Master, to realise that You
          know all.
With You I don't need to act a part,
          pretending to appear other than I am,
          and for that I am very grateful, Lord.

Between You and Me, Lord

RELAX A BIT

WHEN the Bible seems dull and prayer useless we must continue with our daily quiet time, knowing that one day the clouds will disperse and the sun shine again. We must not, however, force ourselves too hard so that we become anxious and burdened.

Stanley Jones tells of a new stenographer he engaged who was determined to do his very best. With that in mind he pressed his pencil so hard on the paper that the whole table began to shake with his efforts. For a few minutes Stanley Jones watched his anxious efforts, then he said to him, 'You will never be a good stenographer if you try so hard to succeed. Relax a bit. Let your pencil glide over the paper and have enough faith in yourself to believe that you will succeed.' That helped. The young man laughed, the strain broke and he became natural.

Hints for Living

THE WASTE-PAPER BASKET

WHAT a splendid innovation, Master,
     is the waste-paper basket!
How necessary an adjunct to successful living!
You who sat by the temple treasury in Your days on
        carth,
     watching the gifts that the passers-by threw in,
do You notice what we consign to the waste-paper
        basket?

That hot scathing letter I wrote, Lord,
     filled with the angry reaction of the moment
        but never sent,
did You nod approval as it was torn up and thrown
        away?

Then the article which would not come right:
the many new beginnings soon scratched out,
others torn up with strong sighs of despair
     or of growing exasperation . . .
Were You sympathetic when I gave up the effort?

You remember that difficult reply, Master,
how I struggled to find the right expressions,
     not saying too much
     yet conveying a meaning?
It seemed impossible to get it finished.
Then I lifted my heart in prayer to You,
     pleading for help,
     and somehow the words came.
The stilted phrase became gracious, the message clear
        but kindly.
As I threw the wasted sheets into the WPB
     I thanked You and felt Your smile.

Into that same WPB I have cast many hopes,
     unfulfilled dreams and longings,
     things that were never to be
and that I could speak to no one about.
     But You knew, You understood.
You helped me to bear silently the keen disappointment.
Thank You, Master.

Between You and Me, Lord

THE MOTLEY CROWD WITHIN

(1) SAINT IN EMBRYO

THERE'S a queer fellow lives within me, Master.
　　　　He calls himself 'Saint in Embryo'.
How much saint there is about him, I don't know,
　　　　but he sure is embryonic.
Sometimes I hardly know that he exists.
　　　　Saint in Embryo leads a hard life, Lord.
　　　　Everything is against him.
　　　　He always has to row against the tide
　　　　and battle with contrary winds.

He will insist on lugging that over-polished halo with him,
　　　　and when he has said something good, really good,
　　　　or done something fine, really fine,
　　　　instead of leaving matters there
　　　　and slipping quietly away,
he spoils things by putting on his old halo,
　　　　which sits at a rakish angle,
　　　　being too big for him.

Lord, he makes himself ridiculous.
Why can't he learn to do good stealthily,
to be good without being puffed up with pride?

I've remonstrated with him about that halo, Master,
　　　　but he says he is forced to wear it
　　　　or people won't know he's trying to be a saint.

When I pointed out that it didn't matter what others thought
　　　　but only what You thought,
　　　　he looked a bit ashamed
　　　　and tried to hide his halo behind his back.
This 'Saint in Embryo' has got a lot to learn, Master.
Will You take him in hand and train him?

2 MAY

(2) BIG ME

TODAY, Lord, has been a bad day.
Big Me obscured my vision.
Not only my vision of other people and their interests,
that would have been bad enough,

81

but worse, Master.
Big Me obscured my vision of You.

This bloated, arrogant Self took the upper hand,
      and I let him do it;
      not with absolute approval,
      but yet with my consent.
Big Me had had a hard day,
he had been ignored, squashed, belittled . . .

      Big Me was furious
      and rampant,
      on the warpath.
And Lord, he blotted You out.
      With his swollen self-importance
      he blurred the outlines of Your face.

I sat in a sacred service.
One of Your servants was proclaiming the rich mercies of
      Your grace;
      I only heard Big Me's complaints.
The congregation sang the triumphs of Your love;
      Big Me drowned their praise with his raucous voice.
Tender verses from Your Book were read;
      Big Me was unmoved.

What can I do, Master, when Big Me takes the reins?
Can You deliver me from his dominance?

3 MAY

(3) SELF-PITY

LORD, there's someone lurking within me:
Shrouded and gloomy she goes her way
      with downcast eyes,
      dragging steps,
      and doleful mien.

She's the shadow of a better me.
She's something good gone sour,
self-replete and self-stifled.

To hear her talk is a revelation;
no one ever had it so bad.
Her setbacks are unrivalled,
her problems mountain-high.

Turned in upon herself she mopes and broods,
      sobs and sighs;
      poor me . . . poor me . . .
      poor miserable me!

Out upon you, traitor, I cry:
I'll have none of your mournful dirges . . .
away with you from my house of life!

Master, give me courage to throw her out:
let me get rid of her once and for all,
and bar the door against her.

Help me to bear bravely my own share of life's burdens;
help me to find others who also suffer
      and try to bring them comfort.
Let me take another's hand in mine and say:
      Courage! the storm will pass;
      look up, day will soon dawn.

Lord, save me from self-pity.

(4) TOUCHY

MASTER, may I introduce Touchy?
I'm not exactly proud of him, I can assure You.
Touchy has lived with me since I was a teenager;
      an unwelcome but most persistent lodger,
      who takes upon himself an old lodger's privilege
      of making himself at home
      and trying to rule.

Touchy has invisible tentacles that stick out in all directions,
with the inevitable result that he's always getting hurt:
      hurt in feelings,
      hurt in his affections,
      hurt in his self-esteem.
He takes offence at the most innocent remark.
He regards every suggestion as a personal affront,
and any criticism as a direct attack.

Lord, it's very unpleasant to live with Touchy.
      I've tried turning him out many times,
      but before I've shut the door on him

he jumps in through the window.
He seems to think he belongs.
I've tried reasoning with him and he says:
    'But I'm so sensitive. You don't understand.'
I've tried laughing at him
    but tears well up in his eyes and he sobs.
I've toughened him up a bit by ignoring him,
    but what a relief it would be
    to get rid of him for ever!

Could you fill me with more of Your spirit, Lord,
so that Touchy would be squeezed right out?

5 MAY

(5) GREAT-AUNT MARIA

GREAT-AUNT Maria is a big trial to me, Lord.
Why need she poke her long nose into everything?
Why should her shadow darken my existence?
    Breathing with every breath I draw,
    inevitably and irrevocably a part of me,
    linking me up in the chain of the generations;
    quirks, foibles, pet aversions, animosities . . .
All these are Great-aunt Maria flowing in my veins.

    Great-aunt Maria didn't like spiders,
    therefore I do not like spiders,
    and my daughter doesn't like spiders;
    so on, ad infinitum.

But that is quite a harmless idiosyncrasy.
There are other things, much more serious:
    tendencies,
    reactions,
    whims and fears,
    strong antipathies,
    all of them part of my built-in mechanism;
    all of them influencing my life,
    colouring my thoughts,
    and affecting my service for You, Master.

Lord, must Great-aunt Maria live with me to the end of
        my days?
Must I be me and yet her all my life through?
Can I never shake off her dominance?

(6) BRAGGART

BRAGGART really is a pest, Master.
He makes me sick when he takes over;
boasting, boosting, embroidering.
  What he is,
  what he's done,
  what he's going to do.
Usch! I'm disgusted with him.
Of course, I know why he does it.
Even a child has that much psychology.
He does it because he feels inferior.

But why should he feel inferior,
just because he isn't like someone else?

Lord, if Braggart would only be himself,
his very ordinary but his best self, all would be well.
You have made us all different,
  because You want it that way, Lord.
We don't need to eat our hearts out
  because we can't sing like A,
  or write like B,
  or talk like C.

I'm always telling Braggart this,
  and basically I think he understands,
but he forgets, Master. And then he starts to brag.
Please forgive him, Lord.
He's not a bad fellow at heart,
but I find it a bit trying at times to co-exist with him.

(7) AN OLD FOGEY

IT'S not very nice to be an old fogey, Lord.
I don't feel an old fogey,
  even if I might look one.
Inside one doesn't feel old.
It's the outside that decays so quickly.

  Lined face,
  sagging muscles,
  greying hair
and young folk class you as an old fogey,
thinking that you have forgotten what it is to be young.

They little know the lively dialogues,
the continued questings,
the voiceless yearnings
that go on under that ageing exterior.

You were never old, Master.
You died in young manhood,
so You never felt the slackening of the life-lines as the
years mounted.
But Your mother stood near the cross, with tired face
and greying hair.

And You loved her,
cared for her,
provided for her.
So You will be compassionate with those of us termed 'old
fogeys', won't You?
Even if we are slow on the uptake . . .
for the will to do still exists when the power to do departs.
The tenant remains youthful while the house decays.
It is Your own law, Master,
and You know best.

8 MAY

(8) NIGGARD

WHAT a mean old fellow Niggard is, Master!
I don't mean only with money, though that is included,
for he was brought up to be careful
and to count his pennies.
You taught that it is better to give than to get, Lord,
but Niggard won't believe that,
or at any rate he won't practise it.
He says that what you keep you have,
and what you give away you lose.
That is why he is so mean.

But money is not his biggest weakness.
His worst fault is that he is so mean with appreciation.
How a compliment sticks in his throat!
To ask him to say 'Well done' to another
would be to risk him choking over the words.
How can I get him to be more generous?
To be quick to say a kindly word,
to jump at the chance to congratulate,

86

to encourage when the going is hard,
to share another's joy.
I shall have to insist, Lord,
stand over him and say: 'Smile!'
take him by the neck and force the issue.

I don't want this old Niggard within me, Master.
Teach me how to outwit him,
to make life so uncomfortable for him
that he will quit for good.

IN A QUANDARY – ALL THESE VOICES

LORD, I'm in a quandary.
What shall I do?
Various voices rise within me and give me counsel,
but their advice is contrary
and I am left perplexed, bewildered.

Great-aunt Maria, old suffragette that she is,
tells me to stand no nonsense, put my foot down firmly,
let them know who they're dealing with.

Big Me sides with her.
Those two are usually allies
when it suits their own interests.
He speaks very forcibly and even eloquently,
pointing out the reasonableness of my objections.
'You have to stand up for your rights,
otherwise people won't respect you.
They'll walk on you,
using you as a doormat.'

Touchy seems very upset, but he snivels so much
I can't understand what he's trying to say.

Then 'Saint in Embryo' breaks in.
Quietly, persuasively,
he argues the other side,
and advises a peaceful, even a pleasant approach.

So what shall I do, Lord? I'm pulled in different directions.
I want to do what is right,
not necessarily in other people's view.
Please, Master, show me what is best,
and give me the courage to do it.

HAVE A GOAL

WHAT shall we do when within us we find such changeable feelings, such ups and downs? We must have a goal and keep it clearly in view. We must do our duty. We must hold on our course even through disappointments and discouragements.

However, we must not do it with clenched hands and tight lips. Watch the marathon runners on TV. They take the course easily, not running as fast as they possibly can, but at a good even pace. In that way they conserve their strength, then as they near the end of the long run, they put all their strength into the last lap.

Life is a marathon race and often an obstacle race. Steadily forward must be our motto, never losing our goal from view, yet never exhausting ourselves so that we cannot continue. If we do lose our breath we must drop out from the race for sufficient time to regain our strength and then recommence from where we are. We must never think of giving up because the course is difficult. The Bible tells us of a cloud of witnesses, heroes and martyrs of old, who watch our progress (Hebrews 11:1–12:2). We, too, must be faithful in our day and generation.

Hints for Living

STEP BY STEP

WALKING is a funny business, Master,
      and so very personal.
One step after another, each step counting,
and each taking one nearer to or further from the goal.

The spiritual walk is also step by step
      by one's own effort.
When You first challenge, Lord,
      the initial response seems exciting,
      a tremendous forward surge into the unknown,
then the pace appears to slacken as the pilgrimage lengthens.

But it is still step by step.
      There is no hitch-hiking in the spiritual life,
      no thumbing a lift with Peter or Paul;
      no chartering a denominational coach,
      or booking a seat
in an ecclesiastical jumbo-jet bound for Paradise.

It would be a lonely business,
      walking the spiritual pathway,

if it were not for Your companionship, Lord.
It's such prosaic plodding at times,
      left foot, right foot, without end,
the first enthusiasm abating while the goal's still out of sight.

Keep me going, Lord,
      keep me persevering,
though at times footsore, blistered, weary.
Thousands of other pilgrims are on their way
      to Your Heavenly city.
Let me greet them cheerily,
      taking courage from their steadfastness,
and may my direction be right,
      even if my pace is slow.

Between You and Me

12 MAY

OLD CLOTHES

DO You mind me approaching You in old clothes, Master?
They are so comfortable and cosy.
      Baggy where they need to be,
      they give easily with movement.
      They are so much part of me
      that I don't need to consider them.

New clothes make me self-conscious and so very careful
      not to get stains or creases.
When I strut around in my new rig-out
      my thoughts revolve around myself.
      How I feel and look,
      how others think I look,
      what impression I am giving.
But when I'm in my old clothes my thoughts are free,
      they fly afar in all directions
      often winging their way to You, Lord.

So You won't mind if I don't dress up to talk to You?
      It's no sign of disrespect
but rather of my great belief in Your understanding heart,
      Your generous acceptance of me
      just as I am
      without frills or fancies.
Thank You, Lord, for that freedom of access.

Between You and Me

13 May

SICKNESS

IT has been said that it is not wrong to be sick, but it is wrong to be more sick than we need be.

Hints for Living

14 May

HEALING

O CHRIST, divine Healer, I would meet with You
      for my need is great.
My body is sick and I long to be well.
I am weary of the pain, the weakness, the depression,
      that seem to shadow my days.
I can't summon up the energy to pray
but I will try to place myself in Your presence.

Master, You who walked the dusty roads of this earth
      in human form,
You know the limitations of the body.
You experienced hunger, thirst and weariness,
yes, wracking pain and ebbing life.
In my thoughts I come to You as though I met You
      at some village well.
You sit there alone as I approach
      and You greet me with a smile.

Soon I am telling You all about myself,
although I judge You know already.
It is a relief to tell You how I feel,
      You have the patience to listen.
I pour it all out, the physical troubles first,
then haltingly my frustrations and setbacks,
      jangling quarrels,
      deep disillusions . . .
What a shattered life I am laying bare before You!

Stretch out Your hand, Master.
Lay it on my head and let me hear: 'Peace, be still,'
      so that my racing thoughts are quieted.
Then speak the word of forgiveness,
so that I may be released from inward tension.
Finally, as I desire to look into Your face,
let me hear You say: 'Be whole!'

Towards You, Lord

HOEING

IT'S just the day for it, Lord!
What a delightful sensation when the needs of the moment
      meet my inward urge to do a job!
Those jaunty tufts of grass mock me with their exuberance
      for they're growing in the wrong place,
      having promoted themselves to the flower beds.
Out with you, I say, as I lop their heads off,
away with you, as I dig their roots loose.
      What a battle in a few square yards of garden!
No wonder the jungle can silently and remorselessly
      encroach on pillared cities,
      engulfing them in rolling green waves,
      strangling them to death.

While I work, I think.
My thoughts circle around the weeds
      that fester and grow in the human heart.
All right, I admit it, Lord, in *my* heart.
Irritations, resentments, self-centredness, envy . . .
what ugly things exist in the garden of the heart.
And just as persistent, just as perennial
      as weeds in the flower beds.
Out with them, I say . . .
      but how to root them out I don't know.
Only You have the power for that, Master.
You must be my divine Gardener
      with Your pruning knife and hoe.
Please get to work on me, Lord.
      Make something decent of me,
something more like what You would have me be.

Between You and Me, Lord

QUICKIE PRAYERS

MOST things nowadays are instant or quickie, so it is no surprise to see a reference to 'quickie prayers'. While they can in no way replace a time set apart for waiting on God, they have their great use in holding a lifeline open between our souls and God. 'Oh Lord, help me' or 'Thank you, Lord' are two good quickie prayers for frequent use.
    I recommend them.

Along the Way

GROWING PAINS

GROWING pains are real, Lord!
People may regard them as an old wives' tale,
      but they are stark reality;
at any rate in teenage thinking and feeling
      if not in an actual physical sense.

Growing up is painful, Master.
It is a comfort to know that You too
passed through the restless adolescent years,
though that was in a quiet country town
and not in the hurly-burly of modern life
      dominated by TV and radio.

To realise who one is, what one is,
      to be aware of deep new urges
      and awesome possibilities . . .
It's quite frightening, Lord!
The tension between childhood and adulthood
      is pendulum-like in its movement;
one day one thing, the next another.

Be my anchor, Master! Hold me fast
even when I sway between conflicting loyalties
and swing and swoop in changing moods.
Keep me on a steady keel,
      a steady spiritual keel,
until the turbulence of the growing years subsides.
Keep my heart centred on Yourself
      until these temporary storms are over
and I enter adulthood's comparative calm.

Towards You, Lord

EACH DAY IS NEW

MOST of us are hampered by memories of the past, memories of things we have done or said or that others have done to us. These incidents lie like heavy weights on us. One secret of successful living is to learn to put each day behind us as it comes to its close.

An American statesman was asked what he thought was the most important rule in life. After some moments of reflection he said: 'To leave yesterday behind and go forward' (see Philippians 3:13b,14).

Hints for Living

COURAGE

IT is not the sudden act of courage on the battlefield that shows a person's character, as much as daily courage against heavy and unchanging odds.

Ur Minnets Gömmor (Down Memory Lane)

MY HANDICAPPED FRIEND

MY friend, Dora, had caught polio as a child, before that disease was really understood and properly treated. Thus her body had grown but her legs remained thin and dwarfed.

As teenagers, we belonged to the same Salvation Army corps and I admired her as she sat in her wheelchair and gave her testimony or sang a solo. Many a time I pushed her wheelchair so that she could get out for some fresh air, for otherwise she was housebound. Then came the wonderful day when she received a mechanical chair which she could herself drive. From that day on she never missed a meeting!

We were good friends, and quite naturally used to discuss all kinds of topics, but I never once heard her complain about her serious handicap. At times I felt rather bad about it for her sake. For instance, when we sat talking we were about the same height, but when I stood up I towered above her, she only coming up to my waist. Yet she would laugh and joke as though there was nothing the matter. I have often wondered what was her secret.

It was clear that she had accepted herself as she was, that she would always be different from others, always bound while others were free. She had shut out any thought of courting or marriage, knowing that was not for her. Whether this acceptance of her hard lot was done once and for all or whether it had to be repeated each new day, I do not know. I only know that she had made a pact with life – to get as much joy as she could from her narrowed circumstances, to allow no bitterness to spoil her days, and to help and encourage others as much as she could.

What a plucky girl she was. That is the kind of person who should be given a medal for bravery.

Dora became a writer, specialising in children's stories. Sunshine and flowers, adventure and fun, all find a place in her writings. There is no sickness there, no complaint, no self-pity. She who cannot walk freely can yet roam the whole world in her thoughts and her pen brings delight to thousands.

Thank you, dear friend, for the inspiration of your life.

Ur Minnets Gömmor (Down Memory Lane)

SELF-ACCEPTANCE

LORD, teach me self-acceptance!
Let me learn to take myself as I am
and not hanker after what I would be.
It seems a failing of human nature –
        that short people want to be tall
        and tall ones try to hide their height.
Why can we never be satisfied?
This is a personal matter, Master,
but you know how I detest my nose . . .
It's just too long for my type of face.
It makes me miserable for I feel folk are looking at it,
        joking about it behind my back
and that makes me unhappy.

Oh dear! I realise, Master, what is happening.
I'm thinking about myself all the time,
        self-centred, introspective, morose;
and in this mood quite unable to see
        that everyone else is pre-occupied
        with their own shortcomings
        and not bothering about me.
How You must laugh at us, Lord!
As if a centimetre more or less on a nose
        could affect a character or destiny,
unless it blinded its owner to the truth:
that what we are within is far more important
        than our appearance.

So keep me sensible about myself, Lord,
even if I wish You had given me more handsome features.
        Keep me from staring at myself in the mirror
        with a longing, a sigh or a groan.
        Let me get on with the urgent matter of living,
by accepting the framework You have provided for me.

Towards You, Lord,

WHEN THE SCAFFOLDING FALLS

SHORED up, Lord!
That's how my life has been,
held by a good steady scaffolding,
        supporting the whole.

Work was a solid scaffolding for many years.
My duties, my interests, my colleagues,
my comings and goings all regulated,
an even routine hemming me in
    yet supporting me
    in a not unpleasant way.
I knew who I was, where I was
    and what I was doing.

Marriage was a pleasing girder
    added to my life.
A comfortable support around me,
    complementing me.
It gave me someone to lean on
    until bereavement struck
    with shattering force.

Good health was a wonderful buttress
    to my activities.
To feel on top of things, to rejoice in doing,
revelling in a sense of achievement
    with almost unflagging energy.
Then sickness came and the pattern changed,
    my own strength seeped away.

The scaffoldings have fallen one by one
    and I have missed them, Lord.
Did I rely too much on them and too little on You?
I fear this is possible for now I feel exposed.
In my need I turn to You, Lord.
You are my strength and stay and You alone.
    Help me to believe it
and to live securely anchored in Your love

God in My Everyday

23 MAY

DANGER AHEAD

DONALD COGGAN, the late Archbishop of Canterbury, threw out a challenge to us all when he declared;

'We live in a welfare state, but there are dangers in being cushioned from the womb to the tomb. The danger is that we may have full bellies, empty minds and hollow hearts.'

Words of wisdom which we should do well to meditate over.

Along the Way

SILENT HEROISM

MASTER, I deeply admire such people!
They seldom make news headlines but the silent heroism
      of their daily lives
brings a warmth of benediction to my heart.

I think of a woman I know
      caring for her husband at home,
lovingly tending his frail body and
sadly bearing with his failing mind.
It is a triumph of enduring love,
      breath-taking in its scope.

I remember a mother with a handicapped child,
not counting the bonds of duty a prison
      but nobly accepting
the surrender of personal freedom.

Such love is like Your love, Lord,
      enduring, outliving
      all rational limits.
It is a portion of divine love sliced from
Your abundant supply . . .
a love that is increased by the very demands
      made upon it,
rather than diminished by the costly toil.

God bless such people today!
I pray for those I know personally
      and for the many unknown
      in like circumstances.
Sustain them by Your presence, Lord!

God in My Everyday

GREENER GRASS

MASTER, it's a human weakness,
      an ingrained human weakness,
to believe that grass is always greener
      a little further off.

How You must laugh sometimes
      when we try to find a picnic spot.

Look! a lovely patch of green . . .
              only to find on arrival that a cow has preceded us.
Over there then! Alas, the verdure is mostly nettles.
Let's try further along!
              No good! It was better back there.

What a picture-story of our approach to life!
The perennial belief that others have it better than we do.
It's envy, Lord, just plain envy,
and an astonishing lack of fact-finding.
Oh, save me from it for it can infect all our being.

One antidote is to be aware of others' problems,
              to make time and give the open heart,
              to listen and learn,
to hear the undertones of stoic heroism,
to realise the sheer bravery of the daily battle
              against adverse conditions,
while to an onlooker all was 'the greenest of grass'.

Help me, Lord, not to be dissatisfied with what I have
and to realise that others have their secret trials and
              worries
              hidden from the world's eyes,
invisible burdens carried with fortitude and touching
              endurance.
Don't let the mirage of 'greener grass'
              tempt me to despise the little plot that is mine,
              to care for and improve.

Between You and Me, Lord

YOU CAN'T MISS IT!

THESE famous words echo in many a motorist's ear after vain attempts to locate a certain building by following intricate directions given by a well-wisher. The trouble is that you can't recognise what you have never before seen.

Unless you know that the shop you seek is hidden behind a huge hoarding, you fail to find it. The station that you 'can't miss', you do miss, because your informant had not said that it lay in a side road.

Once having been that way you would never miss it again, but with an unknown goal ahead, it is not so easy to reach it.

Along the Way

FULL OF WHAT? (WHITSUN)

LORD, I have been meditating . . .
The full vessel runs over with its own contents:
the selfish life drips selfishness,
the loving person spreads love around,
the careless man communicates
        a careless attitude,
heedless of others' feelings, needs or problems.

Lord, I want the overflow from my life
        to be good, helpful and kind.
I pray that what flows out from me
might represent You and not myself.
I know that only what is within can spill over.
No amount of juggling will enable
        a cup full of water
        to drip milk.
And no number of holy phrases
        and cited texts
will pour forth blessing and cheer
if the heart is full of its own goodness
        and not Yours.

Fill me, Lord, with Your Spirit,
so that I have enough for myself
and can overflow into other lives with Your love,
        courage, faith and power;
not consciously by my own act
        but by being used by You
as an irrigation channel to parched souls.

God in My Everyday

TIME-TITHING

A PARSON wrote in his parish notes: 'Why don't you spend one hour in church as a tithe for every ten you spend with radio or television?'

That is quite an idea and might lead to greater congregations. But some of the time used by the mass media presents us with excellent religious programmes which enrich our lives and broaden our experience and for which we can thank God.

Along the Way

UNCEASING GROWTH

IN *A Bridge for Passing*, Pearl Buck wrote, referring to her n⟨
'I need not, I must not, retreat or pause or cease to grow becaus⟨
way alone.' Brave words from a brave woman.

Along the Way

ONE DOT ON A SCREEN

IT overwhelms me, Lord!
My head reels at the immensity of life
and my heart fails as I realise that I am
just one faint dot among millions of others
that appear briefly on the screen of history
            and pass rapidly without a trace.

Do I matter?
That is a vital question for me, Master.
Do *I* matter among so many others?
Does my life count for anything?
I believe it does, Lord, to You,
You, the Creator of life itself, who feel a pang of loss
when the fluttering heart of a sparrow ceases to beat.
You have granted me the gift of life,
            so I believe I matter to You.

Am I reckoning myself too important?
            Pretending that I am making history
            with my brief sojourn on this planet?
No! oh no, but I believe my life counts with You,
that in some way You will weave my days
            into Your master plan.

Let me be available then,
offering myself and all I have and am
            to Your unknown design.
Even if I am an insignificant thread,
            let me not snap
            so that the fabric is weakened.
Let me play my part, however tiny, however obscure,
            towards the good of the whole.
This, Lord, is my humble prayer.

Towards You, Lord

ONE IN A ROW

MY heart is at zero-point, Lord,
>and my spirits are flagging.
I feel desperately alone yet that is just
>what I am not.
I am one in a row of bed-patients.

'This is your bed,' said the nurse kindly,
and I climbed into it with leaden feet.
>*My* bed? For how long?
A frightening prospect of uncounted days
>looms before me.
I lie in total isolation of spirit,
>not alone yet lonely,
with that desperate loneliness which seeps
>into every cell of the body,
>and chills the mind.

From the fortress of my bed,
the only spot which is mine for the time being,
>I survey the scene.
The business of the ward continues,
>voices, laughter, footsteps,
>trolley-wheels passing,
all of them a curtain shutting me in upon myself.
Master, I cling to You now in wordless prayer.
>Take away my fear, quiet my spirit,
let me burst out of this well of misery within
>to find what is positive and good.

The patients on each side of me smile a greeting.
Shall I be as calm as they when I have settled in?
>O help me, Lord!
>I trust in You.
You are with me here just as in my own home.
Let me believe it, even if I do not feel it.
>Let me rest in Your love,
even when I cannot frame a prayer.

Towards You, Lord

THE SIMPLE LIFE

I'M all for the simple life, Lord.
>Just a toothbrush and towel,
>a handkerchief and comb,
>a change of clothes and shoes.

Few possessions, few demands, few worries.
What freedom of spirit when one is not cluttered with things!
What joy in renouncing the chains others forge for themselves!
What delight in simple pleasures:
>the flight of a bird,
>the scent of a rose,
>the soft patter of rain!

What are possessions but ties that bind one to earth,
cords that hamper the soul's free movement?
All this I know and feel, Lord.
But there is one word which upsets my equanimity.
>It is a little word,
>but it is powerful, Master,
>and it occurs so often;
>just four letters
>S-A-L-E.

What magical magnet is hidden in those letters?
The attraction of the simple life fades,
>the joys of the simple life vanish.
I am caught, impaled, tempted beyond my strength,
and I acquire things
>because they appear cheap,
>because they are enticingly presented,
>and skilfully advertised.
Lord, can You deliver me from sale fever?

Just a Moment, Lord

THE DOWNWARD PULL

SOMETIMES we wish that a fairy godmother could wave her wand over us and say: 'From now on you will only want to do what is right, and you will do it happily'. Alas, no! Experience has taught us that there will always be a downward pull within us that we must learn to resist and overcome.

Hints for Living

LOVE-HATE

MASTER, I nourish a strange emotional mixture,
    I have a love-hate relationship,
    a strong but secret love-hate
    directed against a tree,
an old and innocent laburnum.

Most of the time I hate it intensely,
    hate its lopped-off ugliness in winter,
hate its dead flowers spoiling the verdure of the lawn in spring,
Worst of all – its seedpods lie heavily everywhere,
    a poisonous temptation for my grandchildren
and a source of myriads of young plants with obstinate roots
springing up with determined energy.

But when it bursts into golden glory
    for a brief breathtaking display
I forgive it all its faults.
I capitulate to its charms and love it dearly.
I feel proud that its roots are thrust deeply
    into my garden soil,
that its noble head is reared above my fence.

I meditate, Lord, turning my thoughts to You.
There is no love-hate relationship from Your side
    towards us humans.
Your pure love absorbs our gross selfishness,
    swallows up our sins,
    overlooks our shortcomings,
pours itself out a generous stream that sweeps away our
        nastiness
and surrounds us with goodwill and forgiveness.
Thank You, Master.

Between You and Me, Lord

ENJOY SOMETHING EACH DAY (1)

LIFE can run in rather monotonous grooves for some people, particularly the old. We must ourselves create our own moments of joy. These can be quite brief and fleeting but very refreshing.

    The inspiring story of Helen Keller, who could neither hear nor see, impresses me as I read of her remarkable ability to use the sense of touch –

a sense that we appear to have little use for. We rely on sight, hearing, taste and smell, but untold pleasures are open to us in the *feel* of things: the smoothness of a rose petal or of silk, the cushion-softness of velvet, the pattern of lace, the sharpness of a piece of granite.

And the shape of things! To take a vase in our hands and caress its sloping sides, its elegant handle, these are moments of delight.

Search each day for some small thing that can give you enjoyment and I am sure you will not be disappointed.

Hints for Living

COMMITMENT

MASTER, I feel the time has come when I should
    make a definite commitment
    of my life to You.
Up to now I have followed You afar off
but today I want to draw near,
    kneel before You
and acknowledge You as my Saviour and Lord.
You will not repulse me, I know.

What is the strange compelling power
    that You exert, Master?
It is surely because You are alive
    and not simply a legend.
Our human hearts are made with an in-built
    emptiness – a void
that only God can fill.

I have felt this attraction, this call,
this pressure to full commitment for some tune
    and yet I have hesitated.
Now, Lord, I come to You and as far as I can
I yield myself to You – to follow You,
serve You and obey You.

Lord, I remember that knights of old
    knelt all night at an altar
when they made their vows.
    I cannot do that
but may my commitment be as real
    and for life.
So help me, God!

My God and I

MY DUSTBIN HAD A LID

WHEN I carry my garbage down to the neat row of dustbins with their well-fitting lids provided for our block of flats in Helsinki I remember my dustbin adventures in Santiago, Chile.

In Bible days women met at the well. In Santiago we met at the dustcart. In the heat and smells of that crowded city, the uncovered dustcart added its own special odour. When I first arrived I found an old, rusty, dented tin had been left me for garbage disposal. Each day as I heard the dustcart bell ringing, I took my tin out to the edge of the kerb like all the other housewives. It was a matter of waiting for some minutes until one's tin was emptied before returning to the house.

New to South America and patience not being one of my virtues, I decided to put the rubbish out and collect the empty tin later. When I went out to get my lovely rusty tin it had disappeared. Someone had taken advantage of my absence to abscond with it. The only solution was to buy a new dustbin – this time with a lid which gave a little better sense of hygiene. Of course I did not take the lid out to the street. One must be careful not to appear too high-class! But it did useful service in our small, hot backyard, where incidentally I had to do my washing.

My 'washing machine' was a wooden trough on a wooden box. Water had to be heated in the kitchen and carried in pails to the trough. I stood, straw-hatted in the blazing sun, on a couple of bricks and rubbed the clothes on a zinc rubbing board.

My kitchen was simply the passage to the backdoor. There was no window. In winter when the morning temperature was near freezing, it was bitterly cold in that passage kitchen. In summer I nearly collapsed of heat stroke when I tried to cook there. Our adventures in Chile almost seem to belong to another life yet they have a piquant interest without, however, wishing to relive them.

Ur Minnets Gömmor (Down Memory Lane)

ENJOY SOMETHING EACH DAY (2)

HOW the sense of smell can bring back memories! I was sitting one day in the dentist's chair when something she was using brought back a memory of childhood. I asked her if it was camphorated oil, but she smiled and mentioned a technical name.

However, for me the smell rolled away the years.

I saw myself as a child in the bathroom at home. I must have had a cold, for mother was rubbing warm camphorated oil on my chest. It felt so good, mother's gentle hand, the damp heat of the bathroom, the comforting smell of the oil, all combined to make it unforgettable. And there was I reliving and enjoying it years later sitting in a dentist's chair!

Search each day for some small thing that can give you enjoyment and I am sure you will not be disappointed.

Hints for Living

COLOUR

THIS is a paean of praise, Lord,
for one of Your delightful gifts to this world,
        the glory of colour.
I have tried to imagine a black and white world:
black grass and white flowers,
black fruit hanging on black-leaved trees,
black fish swimming in murky waters,
with a blackened sunset at end of day
        heralded by muted twittering of funereal birds.

No! such a world is unthinkable.
In Your generosity, in Your wonderful kindness
        You have given us colour,
thereby enriching our lives a thousandfold.

Thank You, Master, for the hues
        of dawn and sunset glow,
        of myriad-shaded flowers
        and evergreen grass;
for the riotous panorama of spring
        only outdone by autumn's tints.
It's too much! More than we deserve,
        we who litter the meadows
        with our peanut packets, toffee papers
        and empty bags of crisps.
Forgive us all that we add to what You provide
and that our gaudy rubbish spoils Your countryside,
        creating ugly disharmony.

Make us so conscious, Master, of nature's colouring
        that we do nothing to spoil it,
        that we introduce no strident note
        into the blending of Your artistry.
Then with all our hearts we can join
        in a song of praise to You,
        Creator of life and colour.

Between You and Me, Lord

TONGUE ACHE

WOULDN'T it be a good thing, Master,
     if we got tongue ache
when we had misused the gift of speech?
Or if a painful rash spread round the mouth
     when we had told lies
     or uttered cruel slander?
It would at least convince us that we had sinned.
     We get away with so much!
A smile on the face can accompany poisonous words,
     and with a nonchalant air
we can fire a loaded sentence into someone's mind,
starting off a trail of innuendo and suspicion.

Why are we so cruel with our words, Lord,
when we regard ourselves as kind in other ways?
Spiteful words are often lightly said,
     or harsh criticism given,
but what searing wounds, what painful scars, they leave;
breaking up friendships, sowing discord,
creating cliques and rivalries,
often forgotten by the one who spoke them
to live on in destructive power in the hearer.

Forgive the many times I have sinned with my words
     and even if my tongue does not ache,
stab my conscience deeply enough to hurt
     when I offend in speech.
Control my tongue, Master, 'keep the door of my lips'.
Let Your Spirit stand sentry-guard over my utterances.
     Cleanse my inner being,
so that from its source only good and helpful words will flow.

Towards You, Lord

MOTTOES

I LIKE mottoes, either humorous in the style of: 'Always be sincere, whether you mean it or not,' or brief, such as: ' Do it now.'

When a motto catches the eye for the first time, it might have an effect. But what about the 101st time? Better by far to attempt to live with one motto at a time, changing it as its challenge begins to lose its edge. Originating with Dr Grenfell, of Labrador, whose work I admired greatly, the motto I chose when I entered The Salvation Army training college in 1926 was: 'To follow Christ is the greatest adventure in life.'

Now, with my active service behind me, I have changed my motto so as to express the inward longing of my heart for the years that remain: 'To know Christ better; to make Him better known.'

Along the Way

COALS OF FIRE
(Proverbs 25:22; Romans 12:20)

LIVE coals of fire, glowing, hot and searing,
which I would pour on to my enemy's head.
I breathe them out upon him now
    for I am blazing with wrath,
    exploding in anger against him.

But, Master, I know that's hardly what Your Book means
when it counsels us to pour coals of fire
    upon our enemies.
You would have us love them!
Can love ever be like a devouring fire
    which scorches and hurts and maims,
    even consumes its object?
I know the answer to that.

Then what kind of coals of fire can I heap upon
    those who oppose me?
If it is to be fire, it must be something which warms,
    heartens, comforts, brightens,
and the name of that fire is love.
Love expressed in a kind word, a helpful action,
    a friendly attitude, a cheery smile.

By attacking my enemy I cause him to strengthen his position.
By conciliation I weaken his defences
    and enter by a back door
in the hope of agreement and concord.

I will not deny, Lord, that at times
I had far rather burn my enemy than love him,
but help me to go Your way, to try Your remedy,
    for patching up the quarrels
seemingly inherent in human relationships.

Towards You, Lord

DARK GLASSES

A MARVELLOUS invention, Master, tinted glasses
      to counteract eye strain.
You and Your followers knew nothing of that
      as you roamed round Galilee.
Perhaps Your eyes were stronger through less use
      of artificial light,
for an oil lamp gives such a gentle glow.
However, dark glasses are useful, Lord,
      to combat sun glare
and they also tone down unpleasant scenes.

I must beware, though, of wearing dark glasses
      on my soul's eyes.
It would be comforting . . . an easy way out,
not having to confront the full blaze of truth about myself,
or the hard facts of my short-comings.

Unpleasant matters would be toned down,
the shock-glare smoothed from certain acts,
a false green tinting added to dry growth . . .
O Master, it is so easy to be deceived!
Let me welcome the full penetrating light
      of Your gaze
however uncomfortable I feel, knowing that
only You can both diagnose and heal.
      Spiritual dark glasses must be banned!

God in My Everyday

MY POINT OF VIEW

WHAT a lot of disagreements arise from differing points of view on the
same subject! Why can no one else see a matter just as I see it?

I got the answer in an art class.

We gathered round the subject – a lady sitting on a wooden chair – and
we were told to sketch what we saw. My neighbour was quite close to me
yet she saw the model differently, from another angle. Our subject was an
elderly lady who sat with great patience, her wrinkled face bearing the lines
of long experience, her hands quietly folded in her lap.

Some caught her full face, some side face, some partly from the back
with just her profile emerging, the shoulders sagging a little.

Finally the tutor assembled our sketches and pointed out how – with the same model – all were different because of our various standpoints. It was a spiritual lesson to me of how our thoughts of God, Jesus Christ, life itself, moral values and home ties are affected and shaped by our personal viewpoint.

Along the Way

THE ROSE BUSH

I FINALLY accepted defeat, Master,
    that rose bush was dead.
In an excess of zeal I had killed it: by pruning it too hard?
    by watering it too little?
    by moving it at the wrong time?
Who knows?

Its brown and wizened sticks protruding mutely from
    the soil
    voiced a silent accusation against me.
Every time I passed it I felt guilty
but I said to myself: 'These things happen',
and I decided to dig it up and plant a new one.

When the right day came and I arrived
    duly equipped with garden tools,
I stared amazed at the dead rose bush.
The withered stalks still jutted disconsolately upward
    but from their base, from the soil,
    a dark red shoot emerged.
There was still life in the root.

It was then that You spoke to me, Lord,
in such strong tender words that my heart was stirred.
You spoke of hope, of renewed life, of resurrection;
You told of Your power over death and the grave
and with the miracle of the rose bush before my eyes
    it was easy for me to believe.

Thank You, Master,
    for confirming my faith in the ongoing of life
    past death and the grave
    into new expanded being.

Between You and Me, Lord

TOWARDS YOU, LORD

I SAW them this morning, Master,
      tightly clenched praying hands,
lifted in mute worship to a Creator-God.
They were only the new-born leaves of a row of seedlings
      still wrinkled and twisted;
but their fervent stretching into the unknown upper world
      touched me deeply.

They were obeying an inner urge, bewildered yet joyful,
      after having pierced earth's crust:
reaching timorously but strongly upward not knowing
      how far they must go before nature said enough.
Not knowing the storms of rain and wind they would meet,
      the attacks of enemies unknown;
disobeying the law of gravity to fulfil their destiny
      by obeying the higher law of growth.
Hearing nature's call to rise out of seeming death
      to pulsing life, rising sap,
      growth and expansion;
to the final revelation of the hidden bud and seed.

So may I, Lord, respond to that call from You
      which disturbs my heart,
making me dissatisfied with earthly things,
      with finite aims,
and filling me with longings inexpressible
      for something beyond,
something to which You challenge me.
Grant me the pluck to do as the seedlings did,
      to dare to answer,
      confident, believing,
to stretch my hands upward, towards You, Lord.

Towards You, Lord

COMPENSATIONS

LIFE has taught me there are always compensations if you look for them in every circumstance. But life also has smaller compensations, as the woman pointed out who said: 'Ah've only got two teeth left in me 'ead, but praise Gawd, they meet!'

Along the Way

MORE SERIOUS COMPENSATIONS

MY call to Salvation Army officership came with the words of Jesus 'There is no man who hath left house, or brethren, or sisters, or father, or mother, or wife, or children, or lands for my sake and the gospel's, but he shall receive an hundredfold . . . ' (Mark 10:29).

As officers my husband and I faced a life of obedience to farewell orders. If I tried to reckon up how many of these sudden impingements of authority over my pathway brought pleasure, then the score is nearly down to zero yet in every appointment in the eight lands in which we served there was some compensation.

Our biggest shock was transfer from Denmark to Chile in 1949, where we lived in the poorest quarters we ever had – and very little money to manage on. What was the compensation in that house, with its ants, beetles and constant street noise? It was the view from an upstairs window of the mighty Andes mountains bathed in glorious rosy hues at dawn, and reds and purples at sunset. A few minutes at that window each day restored my serenity.

But life's compensations often come as a result of painful experience: sickness, even bereavement. Our hearts by suffering are enlarged and thereby made more alert to others' woes. There is a final compensation for our declining years: 'Though our outward man perish, yet the inward man is renewed day by day' (2 Corinthians 4:16).

Praise the Lord for that!

Along the Way

THE EMPTY NEST

WHEREVER there are children in the family, life is rather noisy and the home is often in disorder. But one by one children grow up and leave the home with quiet and tidy rooms.

For some of us a precious child has left home under other and sadder circumstances. The angel of death has passed and taken a little one to be with God. The place is empty, so empty. The house is still. No more toys litter the floor, no more school-books pile up on the table, no more quick footsteps bound up the stairs.

Is there any comfort for such a loss? Yes, there is. With all my heart I believe that what we call death is only transition, only the opening – and shutting – of a door, and that on the other side of that door is *life,* joyous, full, abounding life, rich in ways unimaginable to our finite minds.

Your child, my child, is there, awaiting our coming.

From my Treasure Chest

19 JUNE

I THANK THEE, SON OF MINE

FOR that sweet, rapturous joy of motherhood
When first thy downy head lay on my arm;
For deepened sense of need for Heavenly grace,
That I might keep thy priceless soul from harm,
        I thank thee, son of mine.

For all thou gavest me through seven short years,
For ringing childish laugh and shining eyes;
For hugs and kisses and dear baby ways,
Thy need of me which made me mother-wise,
        I thank thee, son of mine.

For smiling face when weakness laid thee low,
For pain and sickness ever bravely borne;
And last . . .
For greater understanding of earth's woe,
For sense of kinship with all those who mourn,
        I thank thee, son of mine.

From my Treasure Chest

20 JUNE

MELODIES FROM THE BEYOND

HEAVEN is filled with beautiful music! How do I know it? I heard some of it once and with my whole being I long to hear it again. God granted me for a few moments a thinning of the veil between this life and the next. I did not see but I heard – and how I wish that others, too, could hear what I heard, for it is difficult to describe.

I will open my heart and reveal quite simply what happened.

My first-born, a lovely boy of seven years with blue eyes and fair wavy hair, lay dying of leukaemia. We, his parents, watched by his bedside all night long in our flat in Stockholm. In another room lay our tiny daughter, four weeks old, sleeping peacefully in her cot.

Death . . . Life . . . Why? A thousand whys!

It was over! Our last hope for our son's life had fled. He came to us from God. From our arms he returned to God. Of that we were sure, but the parting was hard. The wound ached and bled in our heavy hearts. I walked from my son's deathbed into the other room, picked my baby from her cradle and fed her. Blessed be duty when the heart sorrows!

Then I heard the music. Soft, delicate, like the quiet plucking of harp strings. I listened intently. It must be the radio, but no, that was not on. Perhaps the neighbour's wireless? I pressed my ear against the wall but no

112

sound came from next door. I walked from one room to the other. Wherever I went the music accompanied me. Then the truth dawned. Those beautiful strains were in my mind. I was hearing them with my inner ear. It was no earthly music; it came from the Great Beyond. The melodies of Heaven. I sat down to listen with my whole being. There was no recognisable melody. There were no chords. Sweet, tender, soothing and joyful, the liquid notes followed one another like the rippling of a stream, continuous and melodious. Of one thing I was sure. Whatever place that music came from was not only beautiful and peaceful, but also *happy*. There was no trace of sorrow in the music. It spoke of pure, rich, undying joy. It comforted, it inspired, it enthralled.

For an hour or so that music sang itself into my heart, lifting me above my sorrow, then it faded and I heard it no more. But I can never forget the wonder of it. Some day I hope to hear it again.

From my Treasure Chest

A LIGHT IN HEAVEN'S WINDOW

THERE'S a light in Heaven's window
Kindled by a Saviour's hand,
There's a Father-heart awaiting
Upon that far-off strand.
Through the maze of earthly windings
Dare I hope to reach that land?

There's a light in Heaven's window
Softly shining from afar;
When the gloom of night enfolds me,
I see God's guiding star.

When at times the darkness deepens,
Shade of selfishness and sin,
God's clear beacon of forgiveness
Wakes hope again within.
Can a wayward, faulty mortal
Life eternal ever win?

There's a light in Heaven's window,
Pledge of God's renewing grace;
This world's darkness cannot quench it,
Its ray a path doth trace.
My heart burns with eager yearning,
Shall I one day see His face?

From my Treasure Chest

WHERE ARE YOU?

MASTER, where are You?
Yesterday I knew.
> Yesterday I rejoiced in Your love;
> Your presence enhanced each task;
> Your comfort filled my heart.

Today, where are You?
> Withdrawn?
> Why, Lord?

Today is empty.
> Today has no joys;
> today has no wings;
> today has no glad future;
all is drear, meaningless.
> Why, Lord?

Has the veil of my flesh thickened so as to shut You out?
Have the shutters of my mind snapped together?
Have I carelessly left the blinds drawn on the windows
> of my soul?

Show me, Master, if the fault is mine.
Help me to put it right,
and, if it is simply a weakness of the earthen vessel that
> bears Your likeness without Your power,
help me still to believe in You;
to hold on in trust until my soul revives.

For I'm lonely without You, Lord,
and without You I cannot live.

Just a Moment, Lord

SELF-DISCIPLINE

SELF-DISCIPLINE is not a popular subject. We feel that we have to pay attention to others' wishes in so many matters that we want to be 'free' to do as we like. But no one attains to a harmonious personality who has not learnt to make rules for himself to live by.

A sensible plan of living, with food, rest, work and pleasure in the right proportions, will help to keep us well.

More and more it is being recognised that a lot of illness comes from wrong emotions in the mind, resentments, hates, fears, anxieties. Only the love of Christ in our hearts can help cleanse us from these insidious enemies of our peace of mind and health of body.

Hints for Living

CREDIT CARDS

CREDIT cards are in fashion, Lord.
Everyone must own at least one
      to be accepted at face value,
a guarantee of money to be paid later.
It is so easy and such a sop to pride!

TV advertisements make it look alluring.
You flourish your card – the waiter bows,
      the bank manager smiles,
      the salesman nods respectfully.
A credit card gives access to the best
      this world can offer.

What have we, Master, to commend ourselves to You?
      To ensure the open door to Your presence
and usher us into the awesome majesty of God?
Here no earthly credit card avails
however much wealth it represents.

But Your Book tells us that through You, O Christ,
      we have access to God
to whom we can come with confidence.
      What a privilege!
      What a priceless possession,
the invisible though real access card gaining us,
      not only entrance,
but a welcome and a hearing when we come
      with our needs to God.

God in My Everyday

A DIFFICULT ART

LIVING is an art, perhaps the most difficult of all the arts, and it requires practice.

Hints for Living

SILENCE

HOW difficult it is, Lord,
to achieve a few moments of silence.
This noisy world presses upon our senses.
Even if we shut off TV and radio in our home
   we hear the distant hum of traffic
   and the vibration of planes overhead.
Some people are so attuned to noise
   that they shun silence as ominous,
whereas it has a healing virtue all its own.

I remember, Master, how You loved
   the silence of the hills
where You withdrew in solitude for prayer.
It was easier in Your days on earth
   to reach open country.
Today our towns spread out like ugly growths
swallowing up green fields and hedges.
For us the solitude of hills becomes
   just a picture on a postcard
or a painting hung on our wall.
Our imagination must place us in the scene.
The silence is perhaps only a few moments
   at dawn or dusk
or stolen between duties.

Help me, Lord, however difficult my circumstances,
to make some brief break of silence daily,
   when I quiet myself before You,
think of Your peace stealing into my heart,
rest in Your love and rejoice in Your goodness,
   without uttering a word.
You will be there and know how to meet my need.

God in My Everyday

SPIRITUAL PIGMY

IT has been said that modern man is an intellectual giant but a spiritual pigmy. Our spiritual life needs deepening. Above all we need to learn the art of meditating on God, that is, quieting the mind before a thought of God, a concept of his greatness or goodness, and thus receiving from Him a touch of divine power.

A doctor has said that the most health-giving thing one man can do for another is to infect him with a vital Christian experience. Those who live in daily contact with God are more likely to be healthy and harmonious than those who live selfish and self-centred lives.

Hints for Living

RELAXATION (1)

BEFORE You, Lord, I sit in silence.
I try to relax my muscles,
        hands and feet,
        head and neck.
I want to be still and know You
        as Your Book recommends.

My thoughts whirl around the usual pattern
        of my day's activities
        so I try to quieten them.
I close my eyes, the better to see You,
        and slow my breathing.
I picture You today as the source of light,
the invisible but potent Light of the world.
Not a blinding searing searchlight
        but a warm golden radiance
        which envelopes me as I sit.
In imagination I let this light play over me,
        bathing me with gentle warmth
which I feel as Your love encircling me.

Master, my heart lifts to YOU in this
        quiet moment.
I believe You are near me. Even more,
        I believe You are *in* me.
Your Spirit within me responds to Your
        transcendent Spirit
who fills the whole universe.
In this moment I feel that I am
        in union with You.
        You in me and I in You.
United, as a branch in the vine with Your life
        flowing into me.
It is a sacred hour.

My God and I

LET THERE BE GRASS

LET there be grass in Heaven, Lord!
My awakened eyes might weary
    of the constant gleam of gold,
and long for earth's cool greening places,
its gardens, moors and meadows.

I've lived in the snowy north
    where all was whiteness,
tiring to the eyes without due protection
but pleasant to the aesthetic sense . . .
diamond glint of frost crystals,
gorgeous blazings of sunrise and sunset,
or purple-blue shadows lengthening on snow wastes.

I've lived in the torrid south
with every green blade scorched from the earth
    for the summer months.
An arid, desert landscape,
life sucked from it for a season until rain again fell.

Hot sunshine every day can become tedious.
So I beg You, Master,
    let there be grass in Heaven!
Grass where small cherubs roll and tumble,
    tired of flying,
and where more mature angels can sit and chat,
or gently twang their harps and sing.
Please, Lord, let there be grass in Heaven,
even if I have to mow it myself.

God in My Everyday

RELAXATION (2)

WE must learn how to alternate periods of work by moments of relaxation. If we remain tensed for hard work all the time, our muscles will tire, and so will our mind. Many people would avoid illness if they could only learn to relax.

However, it is useless to *command* ourselves to relax.

Our tone of authority only causes the muscles to tighten up ready for action.

Hints for Living

BORN GOOD

LORD, it's not fair! Some people are born good,
   docile, even-tempered and placid
   from early morn to late at night,
   from childhood through to old age.
They give me an inferiority complex!
Is their goodness simply a matter of well-functioning glands?

Why should some of us be storm-centres
with low pressure ever hovering on the horizon?
With cyclones brewing and gale winds threatening
and steam blowing off the lid now and again?
   Is it our own fault or can we blame our heritage?

Whatever the cause, what is the remedy, Lord?
At first I seem to hear You say: 'Peace!'
All right, I'll quieten down and listen
   to what You have to say.
'You must be born again . . . born of My Spirit' . . .
Is that the secret of a Christian life?
   Not self-mastery, rigidly exercised,
   a daily clenching of the hands,
an agonising remorse when self-control slips,
but rather a new Master in residence,
   a new life within, controlled by His Spirit?

Then I see some hope for myself, Lord.
I yield myself to You and Your Spirit.
Take the reins of my life into Your hands
   and guide me through each day.
Change and recreate the inner springs of my being
   by Your presence within my heart,
and as the new comes in, let the old self depart, never to reign
   in power again.

Towards You, Lord

CONTROLLED

WE all know what we mean when we say a person is good-tempered or bad-tempered. We are all tempted at times to bad temper and irritation but if we can learn to control ourselves and our moods, we shall be strengthening our character. Or, as the Bible puts it, 'He that controlleth his spirit is better than a conqueror' (Proverbs 16:32).

Hints for Living

OLD FOLKS AT HOME

WE'RE back where we started, Lord, a long time ago,
    just the two of us left at home.
The years in between have vanished so swiftly.
Two young folk setting up their first home in great joy,
    then the exciting arrival of a third.
Pram, cot, baby-clothes, nappies,
    toys all over the place.
The wonder, the sheer wonder of watching a child
    develop,
    rejoicing each day over some new progress,
    marvellous miracles of growth . . .
    a smile, a tooth, a word, a step.

Then another baby . . . and another.
The house is full of noise and movement,
laughter but also tears.
There is a pause for silence as a child's coffin
    is carried down the stairs . . .
    but life must go on.
Building bricks give place to bicycles,
    school satchels are full of books
and children become suddenly worldly-wise.

Then one by one, as they came, they go,
    taking their own belongings with them.
There's more room now that the nest is empty of young.
At first there is a great hollow echoing . . .

Almost without realising it we've become the old folks
    at home.
    Children and grandchildren come to visit,
    fill the house for a few hours with activity
    then depart leaving abrupt quiet.
Peace! The gentle peace of inner harmony,
    Your gift, O Master, to the humble heart.
Let Your radiance shine upon the two grey heads
    at the hearth,
    for they are content with what has been
    and grateful for Your companionship.

Between You and Me, Lord

MY BIGGEST FEAR

MASTER, I can't put it into words . . .
    It is a haunting phantom lurking in the shadows
       of my life, hidden from all but You.
You already know my biggest fear, that my mind
    should wear out before my body.
There is a word for it but I will not whisper it, even to You.

You did not live so long, Lord, that this became Your problem.
The threatening symbol in Your life was a cross,
    a felon's cruel death.
and You met it in young manhood.
We of today live much extended lives,
cushioned from cradle to coffin by a helpful State,
and the way can be very winding and long,
    tedious towards the end.

We who face the problems of the latter years,
when frailty replaces energy, memory starts to fail
and hearing and sight diminish, what word have You for us?

It comes so crystal clear, so convincingly true:
'Lo, I am with you all the days, even unto the end.'
We know that the physical envelope in which we live
    will become old, wrinkled and worn
    as it travels through the avenues of time,
but the letter inside is safe, vocal and clear
and it will reach its destination
    with no single line deleted.

Towards You, Lord

ART

ONE of my New Year resolutions was to attend art classes. All my life I have hankered after a chance to do oil-painting without knowing whether I had any gifts in that direction, so for the past few months I have enjoyed dabbling in colour. I haven't produced any masterpieces, but the effort has been very rewarding. I have learnt a new way of seeing with something of the artist's sharpened appraisal of colour and shape, texture and shading. How rich in interest this old world of ours is!

What a pity that we go through life so blind to many of its simple and lasting pleasures!

Along the Way

MARTYRDOM

MARTYRDOM has its pain, Master,
      but it also has its pleasure;
the subtle satisfaction of nursing a grudge,
      gloating over it,
      magnifying it,
building it up from a brick to a high-rise tower
      where it dwarfs all near it.
That pleasure, that sneaky selfish pleasure, I have known.

It's nothing to boast about, Lord,
this ability to wear the martyr's crown at the
      slightest opportunity,
noting with dulcet joy the regret on others' faces,
      hearing the concern in their voices,
while all the time one wears a patient, resigned air.

True martyrdom has none of those delicate delights;
one person suffers while the rest gloat;
but in false martyrdom all around suffer
while one revels in self-pity, in breast-hugging
      abasement
      and in stealing the limelight, however sickly its beam.

Lord, the true martyr's crown is not for me,
but in Your mercy, in Your boundless mercy,
      save me from the false kind.
Save me in spite of myself and my baser leanings,
pull me up with a start when I begin to think myself
      badly done by,
      overlooked, overworked or unappreciated,
when little devils of temper whisper in my ears:
      'It's a shame how they treat you!'

Master, teach me to speak out at such moments,
not hotly but rationally, if I feel I am put upon.
Deliver me from smouldering resentment which can
      burst into a blaze,
      enveloping me with flames
and creating a spurious martyr's stake on which
      I burn,
      consumed from within myself.

Between You and Me, Lord

KITTY WAS MISSING

AS a young Salvationist, on Sunday afternoons I led a class of girls, some of whom had already left school and started work. One of those was Kitty, a nice girl with a round, merry face and curly brown hair who came *every* Sunday and seemed to enjoy it.

One Sunday she was missing – perhaps she was sick or had a cold? Well, I would call round next evening after work. But something within me seemed to insist, 'Go today. Go now!' I tried to push the feeling away for there was so little time between afternoon and evening meetings. Still the inward voice insisted, 'Go now!' I decided to call at her home, even if it meant missing my tea. Kitty's mother came to the door. Her eyes were red with crying, but she brightened up as she saw me, saying she had hoped that I would come.

I followed her in and found Kitty, also in tears. After a time, the whole story came out. A week earlier Kitty had started to serve in a shop. It was at a time of depression and jobs were not easy to find. One day as she put money into the till, a sudden temptation overtook her and she slipped a bright silver coin into her pocket. From behind a curtain the shop owner had watched his new assistant and now he had caught her in a theft. She was dismissed on the spot.

It was not simply the loss of her job which upset Kitty, but the realisation that she, a professing Christian girl, could fall for a sudden temptation. She had wanted to come to Sunday school and confess to me, but her mother had said that she must remain home as a punishment.

In my youth and inexperience there was little I could say, but I prayed with Kitty and her parents, promised to try to find her another job, and I believe I left the little family somewhat comforted.

I was always glad that I had heeded the inward pressure of God's Spirit to go immediately to Kitty's home.

Ur Minnets Gömmor (Down Memory Lane)

RELAXATION (3)

SOME of my readers will already have their favourite ways of relaxation, but others may be interested in this advice. 'Think of yourself as a sack of potatoes, tied with a string. Cut the string mentally, see the potatoes roll out, and think of yourself as the empty sack'.

Rather a long way round to achieve relaxation! You may prefer to do as a cat or dog does, stretch and wriggle until comfortable, then drop all your worries and enjoy the next few minutes.

Hints for Living

NOISE

NO transistor broke the silence of your Galilean hills, Master.
    When You left the crowded village
    and sought the stillness of the heights,
    you could hear the twitter of birds,
    the hum of insects,
    the soft swish of the wind through tufted grass,
    and in the silence God could speak to You.

But I live in days of tension, of speed, of noise.
My generation is afraid of silence,
afraid of listening, in case they hear . . . nothing.

We are keyed up to noise, drowned in canned music,
persistent voices pursuing us the round of the clock.
Is it any wonder that we are tense and nervy?

In Your Book the seer tells of silence in Heaven
    for what seemed half an hour.
    Blest break in the celestial chanting,
    welcome pause in the Heavenly harmonies:
    A whole half hour . . . deep, satisfying silence,
    something to look forward to
    when earthly noise grates harshly on the ear.

In the meantime, Lord, help me to draw within myself,
    stilling myself in the silence of my soul;
    there finding strength and refreshing,
    shut off from the world's jarring noises
    for a few brief moments at a time.
    A quiet oasis in a desert of sound.
    There in that silence
    I shall meet with You and again be strong.

Just a Moment, Lord

HABERDASHERY

WHAT a delightful word that is! I had quite forgotten it until recently, when directed to 'haberdashery' in a large department store. It took me back to my childhood when I was sent to 'the haberdasher's' for some cotton and tapes. There seemed to be something very mysterious and enticing about a shop with that name. Prices of articles were written in a kind of monetary shorthand which only the shop assistant could read, although I did work out that three little dashes at the end meant three farthings. What complicated prices ruled in those days! One and eleven pence three-farthings, one pound nineteen shillings and eleven pence three-farthings. Whatever the price it seemed to end in three-farthings, but sometimes the shop assistant had no farthing change to give, so instead the customer was proffered a row of pins stuck into paper.

Strange memories from the past conjured up by the sound of a word!

Along the Way

POSTCARDS

PICTURE postcards lie, Master,
or at best give only part of the truth
      in the scene they depict.
However attractive the place may look
one can be sure that it is shown
      from an advantageous angle
      in the best possible light
      and on a sunny day,
possibly the one sunny day that month!

Waving palms and a blue swimming pool
      look very enticing on a card,
though they wake a sharp stab of envy
      against the sender.

It is good, then, to remind oneself
      that postcards convey only the rosiest vision.
They don't show the stinging flies,
      the buzzing mosquitoes
      or the creeping ants.
They don't convey the unpleasant smells
      and the blatant noises.
They are one-sided and deliberately over-optimistic.

Lord, save me from postcard mentality,
      always believing the glamorous,
      the super-coloured and glossy,
and comparing it to the detriment of my more plain
      and humdrum life.

Keep me from imagining that the exotic is *real* life
and my usual duties but a treadmill to be escaped from.
Let me find some joy, Lord, in the everyday.

Between You and Me, Lord

ONLY ONE

LORD, You have promised to be where two or three meet.
That thought has been an inspiration to many.
But I am neither two nor three,
> I am only one.
> Is Your promise for me too?

I remember Nicodemus coming to You at night,
> creeping stealthily up the steps
> to find You alone.
> To him You opened Your heart,
> and he went out into the dark a changed man.

I remember the woman at the well.
> You asked her for a drink.
> It was a kindly way of making contact.
> And then You spoke to her,
> showed what her life had been
> and what it could be;
> that day she would never forget.

So I take courage:
though I am alone, I do not need to feel lonely,
> to brood over the stings of life,
> to consume my own smoke
> or to bear alone a weight of sorrow.

I, too, can meet with You. I can share with You,
share my secret hopes and fears,
> talk out my distresses,
> ventilate my problems,
> and know that You understand
> and love me.

Just a Moment, Lord

HOLIDAYS

MANY of us are looking forward to holidays of one kind or another, and particularly for ladies a most burning question is one of clothes. What shall I wear? About the best holiday advice I ever heard is the following:

'Think out carefully how many clothes and how much money you will require, then take half the clothes and twice as much money and you will be all right.' I guarantee that is sage counsel.

Along the Way

BOXES

I'VE been turning out some old cardboard boxes, Master.
They've lain for a long time on cupboard shelves,
so long that I've almost forgotten what they contain.
    I'm amazed at what I found.

Why ever did I put away those objects
    as something worth keeping?
They might once have been useful or ornamental
    but their day has passed.
I look on them now with keener appraisal
    and with rather mocking disregard
    for my former decision to keep them.

Those souvenirs of a trip abroad . . .
While the holiday was fresh in my mind
    each item was a thrilling memento
    calling up happy moments in unfamiliar scenes.
Now the glamour has gone from them
    for the memories are fading.

Jumble sales, white-elephant stalls . . .
such must flourish with what were once treasured possessions,
    prized for a time
    then put away and forgotten.

I wonder, Lord,
    will it be like this in the Beyond
    when we look back on our earthly life?
With new understanding shall we be amazed
    at the irrelevance of much that gripped our minds
    and filled our hours?
Perhaps we shall then comprehend how often You could not,
    or would not, grant our requests.

Between You and Me, Lord

STAY-AT-HOMES

IF unable to get away for a holiday this summer I hope you will make small breaks for yourself out of the ordinary routine, even if only through a thrilling book or a new hobby. May you be refreshed in the Lord, resting in his care, lifting your heart to him in matters great and small.

Along the Way

TEMPTATION

MASTER, it is encouraging to learn
    that You too were tempted
    during Your years on earth.
Had You not had that experience I might come to You
    with less hope of being understood.
Temptation seems so *soiling*, Lord!
It leaves a stigma on the spirit, a smirch in the mind,
    a sense of unworthiness and of being unclean.
None of this can be true, Master,
since You were tempted yet without sin.

Here is my problem, Lord.
How can I distinguish between being tempted
and myself plotting some wrongdoing?

Both seem to start in the mind with stray thoughts
    forming into plans.
At what moment can I recognise and reject them?
Would that I had a sentinel on guard
    who would sound the alarm
when spiritual danger was near.
I have, Lord! I realise that Your Spirit
will warn me of approaching evil
if I yield myself under Your control.
Thank You for that! And help me, Lord,
not to be downcast when tempted,
for it is part of spiritual growing
    towards maturity.

God in My Everyday

EMPTY STICKS

THIS morning a chubby, small boy preached a wordless sermon to me. As I passed he held up an empty ice-cream stick for my inspection. All gone! Nothing left but a slight stickiness of fingers and lips. Was he asking for pity . . . or the wherewithal to buy another?

He must learn, as must we all. You can't eat your cake and still have it. He chose to buy and eat. He has the memory, the taste for a few minutes, and then . . . the empty stick. One of the problems of life is to know what to do with our empty sticks, the leftovers of what once was. We can go round showing them to others in the hope of eliciting sympathy or generosity, or find a waste-bin and dispose of them once and for all.

The choice we make has a curious relationship to our happiness a our usefulness. May the Lord teach us to enjoy fully when there is something to enjoy and to hide our hurts and disappointments in our own breast. Save us, O Lord, from wallowing in self-pity and from telling others the dismal tale of what ought to or might have been, or once was. Give the courage to throw away our empty sticks . . .

Along the Way

YOU TOOK ME TOO SERIOUSLY

YOU took me too seriously, Lord.
When I said I would go anywhere for You,
I didn't mean a place like Blackpoint.
> It's obvious that I couldn't go there.
> You understand that, don't You?
> The climate is damp, so I might get rheumatism;
> then the houses are built in long rows,
> long, monotonous rows,
> and living under those circumstances
> might cramp my individualistic style.

I am quite willing to go anywhere for You, Master,
> with certain reservations.
I just want this to be clear between ourselves
so that You don't ask me to do anything that is
> beyond my normal capacity,
> contrary to my usual custom,
> or infringing on my personal rights.

Then when I said I would give You my all,
> it was just a figure of speech.
> I trust You understand it like that.
> It was poetic language,
> an exaggeration for the sake of making a point,
> not a statement of fact.

I know I should give and be and do all for You, Lord,
> but I simply haven't got that far as yet;
> perhaps one day I might.
> I know I ought to, but still . . . You see . . .

Just a Moment, Lord

129

A NEW DAY

A NEW day has dawned!
Master, I want it to be a day
      spent with You.
As I drew back the curtains
      I lifted my heart to You,
asking Your blessing upon the hours ahead
and committing myself once more
      into Your care.

What a difference such a beginning makes
      even to the most humdrum day.
The moment of prayer is an act of worship,
      a linking on to You, Lord,
a step of faith before the unknown ahead.
Remembrance of that act of dedication
      casts a warm glow over duties
and tightens up any spiritual slackness.

Can any period of twelve hours
      be a new day?
Isn't today much like yesterday?
      It need not be.
Each dawn brings new possibilities,
      new challenges,
      new evaluations,
if only I am alert enough to see them.
So let me brace my spirit by saying:
      'This is a new day;
it can be a good day with Your help, Lord.'

God in My Everyday

FLORENCE ALLSHORN

I WAS greatly impressed when I read the story of Florence Allshorn, a missionary nurse for many years in India. She came to a hospital where the head-nurse was a hard, demanding type, whom everyone feared. One day Florence sat crying on the veranda when an Indian helper came by and said, 'I know what is the matter. Other nurses before you have met the same difficulties. You come out here with the message of Jesus Christ who can meet all our needs, but he doesn't seem able to help you.'

The young nurse pulled herself together, spent hours in prayer and found a way of co-operating with her difficult superior. Later, Florence became head of a college in England which trained women missionaries.

Do you know what she reckons is the most important lesson of all to learn? How to get on with other people different from you.

She learnt her lesson the hard way, but then was able to teach others how to conquer.

Putting God and His Kingdom first, one can find the solution.

Hints for Living

TRANSLATIONS

MASTER, You learned to speak at Your mother's knee
in the ordinary language of the day,
yet Your words come down to us through
        the pages of Your Book
in many different translations.
Translations which are quarrelled over,
        compared and disputed,
        admired or criticised,
        accepted or rejected,
with one crying: 'I am for Ancient'
and the other countering: 'and I for Modern'.

We have lost the sounds You spoke, Lord.
The soft winds of Palestine bore them away
        but the meaning lived on
in the hearts of those You chose to be with You.
We are now so far off in time that we are
        dependent on translators
to mediate Your message to us.

O Jesus Christ! Help us to grasp Your message
even if the frailty of human transmission
shows faults in the actual phrase-making.
You translated God to us by Your life
        and Your death.
You translated the divine search into human terms
and showed what life might be,
        permeated by Your Spirit
and lived under God's control.
Let my heart be open to Your message
through whatever medium it comes.

God in My Everyday

THAT AWFUL RECORD

THERE'S an awful record playing, Lord,
 playing all the time.
I can't get away from it,
I can't deafen my ears to it,
 for it's in my own mind, Master.

Now You made my mind and You know its workings.
It's a fine piece of mechanism which You have created.
Why then should it play over and over again silly incidents
 which I want to forget?
 Over and over, Lord,
 until in irritation I say: 'Shut up!'
But my mind won't shut up, Lord.
It goes on churning over the same old grievances,
 the same old petty grudges,
 and I don't like it.

You made my mind, Master.
But I suppose that I must accept responsibility for what
 I have put into it.
Certain things have made deep grooves and the needle sticks,
 just there, and there . . .
Lord, I'd like to break that old mental record;
 smash it,
 throw it out,
 be free from it.
But how can I, when it is in my own brain?

Is it possible that part of me enjoys its self-pitying meanderings
 and that is why I can't get rid of it?
Master, will You show me how I can deal with this
 enemy entrenched within me?

Just a Moment, Lord

LENGTHENING VISION

I HEARD a boy telling another of how his sight had improved after
treatment and how he was now able to see much further than before. It was
quaint to hear this lad of about 12 saying 'When I was young . . . but that
was how he started. 'When I was young I couldn't tell the difference
between a sparrow and a blackbird, as it was simply a blur. Now I can
recognise birds by their colour and size.'

Then he added a significant statement which I pass on to you: 'My vision has lengthened as I have grown older.'

His reference was simply to his eyesight, but I took it as a spiritual aspiration and prayer, that my vision might lengthen as my days pass.

Along the Way

THE VISION

WAS it a vision or the result of deep thought?
For a few moments I seemed to pierce some veil
where before me lay the whiteness of Your purity,
  Lord,
  the absoluteness of Your truth,
  the fullness of Your joy,
a pathway broadening into ultimate fulfilment.

Behind me lay the shadows,
  deepening into black nothingness,
into which I fain would slink to hide my stains
  and my threadbare self-righteousness.

I dared not turn back, Lord, though desperate my plight.
Towards the light my very need impelled me,
towards that blinding whiteness
  which revealed my sins in painful clarity
  yet absolved them in merciful charity.
Closer I felt I must press to that stern truth
  that pierced my subterfuges
  yet offered the only real security.

On, on, I felt I must go on . . .
I daren't retreat to the beckoning darkness.
Once having seen Your purity, love, truth and joy,
  I longed to possess and be possessed.
Cost what it may, I knew I must advance,
for only You, Master, could satisfy my soul-hunger.
  Forward I must struggle.

The vision faded . . .
I was back in the everyday,
but something remained, a strong insistence,
  that I must never give up the effort
to reach the heights that You had shown me, Lord.

Between You and Me, Lord

INDWELLING

YOU indwell us, Master . . .
What do You get out of that?
      A lot of problems,
      a lot of heartache . . .
It is love's nature to want to be
      with the beloved.
'I in You' is the creature seeking the Creator
      of necessity
      for help and support.
'You in me' is divine condescension,
      a limiting beyond all belief.
I get the advantages, You the disadvantages.

Why do You do it, Lord?
      I know the answer.
You do it because of Your great love,
      Your overwhelming compassion.
Your recorded incarnation in human flesh
      is repeated daily
as by Your Spirit You indwell us today.
But at what cost to Yourself!
You meet choked channels of expression,
      narrow views and prejudices,
      lack of courage, faith and joy.
These are the bonds with which we bind You,
      free Spirit of the eternal God.
Forgive us that when we ask You to indwell us,
      we are such poor hosts.
Blaze Your way into our hearts, Lord,
      burning away the hindrances,
expanding us even beyond our own desires;
creating the climate where You can express Yourself
      through our feeble humanity.
      Do it now, Lord!

God in My Everyday

SPIRITUAL VITAMINS

HAVING been presented with a copy of a calendar which contains a text for each day of the year, I have hung it on the kitchen wall and each day I read the short text as a morning stimulant, something I can turn over in my thoughts as I go about my tasks until I have time for my daily devotions. Much inspiration can come from a brief text.

Along the Way

SPARE PARTS

ARE there spare parts for the spiritual life, Lord?
When faith in God's love has worn thin,
> when trust in God is shattered,
when the lamp of hope flickers faintly . . .
Are spare parts available, Master?

Can living saints be donors to needy sinners?
> Offering a tender conscience
> a responsible mood
> a prayerful acceptance
> a strongly-built faith
out of their spiritual abundance?

I ponder these questions before You, Master,
and it seems to me that the answer is yes!
There *are* spare parts for the spiritual life
proffered through Your abounding mercy
> poured out in rich streams
> from the treasury of Your grace,
> and only awaiting acceptance.
And saints can be donors to modern prodigals
> through earnest, believing prayer,
through humbly and joyfully witnessing to what
> God has done for them.

> So no one need despair,
however blank their present experience,
however low their spiritual temperature,
however hopelessly they regard themselves.
> Spare parts are available!
> Praise God for that!
Shake off the old broken scraps of faith,
tone up the soul's sagging muscles.
Brace your will for a new commitment.
> Ask your Maker for what you lack
> and stride forward bravely.

God in My Everyday

135

MAKE ME REALISTIC

MAKE me realistic, Master.
Let me define terms to myself.
I know I need a greater love for souls,
but what are 'souls', Lord?

Help me not to think of them as
        feather-light, clinic-clean wraiths
        floating invisibly around;
        interesting because unidentified,
        loveable because unknown.

Help me to remember that 'souls' are just people:
        old bodies with smelly breath and irritating ways,
        youngsters decked out in long hair and tight pants,
        children with runny noses and grimy fingernails,
        rich old ladies nursing lapdogs, and many others.

Keep me, Lord from praying for souls in general
        while ignoring my nearest neighbour.
Don't let me kid myself that I love souls
        when I can't stand the sight of Mrs Smith.
        Mrs Smith is a soul,
        doubtless a very skinny, undernourished one,
Squeezed almost out of existence by a fat, over-nourished
        body,
        but nevertheless a soul, a needy soul.

Make me realistic, Lord.
Open my eyes to the fact that love for souls is simply
        caring about people.
It's harder put like that, Master.
        Souls are comfortably distant and abstract;
        people are uncomfortably near and substantial.
It's almost a pity that I see it so clearly now,
        for I'll have to do something about it.
I'll try.
I really will,
I promise You, Lord.

Just a Moment, Lord

SPACES

RECENTLY I was given an unusual book. It had a sketch and just a few words on each page, with plenty of white space showing. I found the book very relaxing, and inspiring. One had time to absorb, to think. It reminded me of the poet's line:

'Let there be space in your togetherness.'

We all require 'spaces' around us at times, so that we can get to know ourselves, become integrated and recover our poise. Even husband and wife, or the best of friends, require 'spaces in their togetherness'.

Along the Way

FACES

I AM fascinated by faces. Two eyes, a nose and a mouth, yet infinite variations on the same theme. It is not the features that interest me, but the expression.

Such a lot is stamped on the face. Some young faces reveal surprising bitterness. The hard lines of the jaw and lips are outward signs of inward conflict. The same features would be attractive if only they were softened. A young mother, still good-looking, is tired and jaded. When she droops she ages visibly by several years. Making ends meet can be harassing. Then a friendly neighbour stops her to chat and her face lights up. She continues her shopping in more cheerful mood. Courage comes back to her heart and the tension fades from her face. Peace is a wonderful cosmetic.

Old faces are very attractive. The chisel of time has grooved deep lines on brow and cheeks. Marks of experience. Twin vertical furrows between the eyes tell of pain and anxiety, sorrows of the past, burdens patiently borne. Sagging mouth muscles give a stamp of weariness, of seeming depression, but then the face lights up and is transformed.

A gleam of fun makes the eyes sparkle, and laughter lines crease easily across the temples in well-worn tracks.

Along the Way

THE BLIND MAN

THANK You, Lord, for the words exchanged
  and the exhilaration they brought me.
The heavy traffic rumbled past,
  filling our nostrils with petrol fumes
as we patiently queued at the bus stop.
Alerted by his white stick
  I entered into conversation.

'Wasn't the traffic noisy?' was my first venture,
but he countered it with a nonchalant:
  'I don't notice it.
I fix my mind on other things,
green fields, flowers and leafy trees.
In that way I escape the present.
It's a good solution,' he chuckled.

And that was a blind man's reaction
  to a tiring and long wait.
I realised I was in the presence
  of a philosopher of great worth.
What a lesson he taught me!
What insight he gave me into the secret
  of a serene mind.
There was I, with all my senses unblunted,
feeling aggrieved at having to wait;
whereas a sightless man could point the way
  to inner harmony.

We boarded the bus and sat together,
  continuing our conversation.
When I left him I thanked him sincerely
  for having given my spirit a lift.
Master! at times I grumble at much smaller setbacks
  than the loss of sight.
Help me to learn the blind man's secret of living
  with inner resources ever at hand.

       Towards You, Lord

HEDGES

I SAW it so clearly, Lord,
Through the words of one of Your servants.

I have built hedges around my life
      without realising it.
Higher and higher they have grown
      without my knowledge.

These hedges have shut others out
      and myself in.
It was comfortable so, comfortable and cosy.
      Less demanded of me,
      less expected of me,
      only myself to consider.

I have hedged about my time. *My* time!
Did I create time to be my own?
Have I sovereign right to twenty-four hours a day?
Is not each hour a token of Your grace?

I have hedged about my leisure.
      My free time is my own, I have said,
      and I have miserly gloated over it,
      resenting any encroachment upon it.

I have hedged about my love.
      These, and these only, I care for,
      my nearest, my dearest, my friends,
      all precious because they are *mine.*

Forgive me, Lord. Forgive my selfish living,
      my self-centredness,
      my disregard of others.
Help me to tear down the high hedges I have built
and in their place to plan an open garden.
      Then I can look out
      and others can look in
and we shall be drawn nearer to one another.

Just a Moment, Lord

CRITICISM

CRITICISM is unpleasant, Lord.
It is bitter medicine, administered often by a careless hand,
and it can smart and sting long after.
Why is it that all criticism seems unjustified?
Is it because we feel affronted when our
        personal territory is invaded?
We are like an indignant bird,
        angrily defending our garden path
        with squawks and fluttering wings;
or like a wild animal circling its domain
        with surly mien and warning growls.
Criticism we see as an enemy to be kept at bay.
        After all, we know best!

There's the rub, Master!
We see from within, others see from without
        and therefore opinions differ.
Where can the truth lie, Lord? Somewhere in between?
Can I never be right because I see everything
        from my own angle?
And are others always wrong when they see the matter
        from theirs?

Master, help me not to flare up when criticised.
Help me to search for the grain of truth
        hidden in the unpalatable words,
        making up my mind to profit by it,
and to throw away the rough chaff in which it was
        embedded.
Then even my enemies will be doing me a good turn,
        Lord,
        by showing me where I can improve,
and that is something to be grateful for.

Towards You, Lord

WALKING MEDITATION

I HAVE always found that walking helps thinking and thus aids prayer. It need not be in lonely countryside either, though the natural surroundings help to raise the spirit.

If the weather is bad it can even be up and down the sitting-room.

Presumably the movement helps the circulation and the extra blood available clears the brain. The benefits of the kneeling, standing or sitting posture for prayer have often been discussed and each has its adherents. But walking prayer is to my mind very helpful. Many a trudge to the station or the bus or shops can be over holy ground as we lift our hearts to God in simple, earnest petition.

Along the Way

COURAGE FOR TODAY

LORD, give me courage for today!
I dare not look ahead into the vista
     of far-stretching time
     or tomorrow's tasks,
but for one day, this single day,
     grant me courage, Lord.
Courage to tackle the duties to be done,
courage to face the people I must meet,
courage to hold my head high though I quail.
     Grant me quiet courage, Lord.

Let me show a brave face despite inward desolation,
     the sudden panic of aloneness,
     fears for the future,
or simply a nameless dread that grips me
     with cold clammy hands.
Grant me courage for today, Master.

Just for this day, Lord, grant me sustaining grace,
     strength for each hour that comes,
     valour when my heart feels faint;
may I sound plucky when my nerve fails.
Let me reach the evening hours having won through,
     perhaps not gloriously,
     yet adequately.
Let the thin thread of my endurance stretch
     to its utmost limits,
because it is strengthened and sustained by You.

For this one day, Lord, I pray.
     Help me through it,
and when night comes I shall thank You
     from a grateful heart.

Towards You, Lord

ADVICE

LORD, this morning I asked advice
    on a small practical matter
    from one I considered an expert.
Then, as directions were given, I heard myself inject impatiently:
'Oh yes, and so and so . . . I know how to do it!'
Afterwards I was confounded.
    Why hadn't I listened,
    held my peace
and received what I had asked for?

It is the same, Master, when I seek Your guidance.
I babble on about not knowing what to do
    with the choice of alternatives.
    I could do this . . . or that . . . which is best?
I don't *listen* to what You have to say.
I need to ask You so often for advice, Lord,
    but help me,
when I have put my case, to wait . . .
    waiting for Your guiding words
or else a nudge from You in the right direction.

Sometimes in the past I don't seem to have received
    any guidance on my problem
    even when I have waited on You.
Then I have tried to leave the matter for the moment.
Perhaps the time is not ripe for a solution . . .
Perhaps I must learn a lesson of patience.
While I am waiting, events are nevertheless moving
    imperceptibly but surely
towards making my way clear.
What a lot You need to teach me, Lord!

My God and I

PRICK OF CONSCIENCE

THE crush in commuter trains presents
    its own problems, Master.
How far can one exert one's rights
    and push for a place?
I was a standing passenger, although
I had paid as much as those who sat.

We were packed in like the proverbial sardines,
yet many of us were trying to read books
or newspapers.

With one hand clutching the strap and the other
holding my book open
I tried to concentrate on my reading.
It suddenly dawned on me, Master, that
while I was getting the light on my page ,
my shadow threw one of the sitters into shade.
She too was trying to read!
With inward satisfaction I thought:
'You've got the seat but I've got the light!'
It pleased my sense of justice.
I rather gloated over it.

Then my conscience pricked me, for I am a Christian.
I managed to turn slightly so that a gleam of light
shot past me on to her book.
Did she look up and thank me with a grateful nod?
Not likely!
She was probably unaware of my action and oblivious
of the halo which I now felt encircling my brow.
A silly little incident, Lord?
Yes, it was
but I'm glad You gave me that mental prodding
to change my attitude.

My God and I

GREAT EXPECTATIONS

ONCE, when we lived in Sweden and my children were small, I had been
away on a visit to my parents-in-law, who then lived at some distance. On
my return there was a lot to tell and I did not forget to say that Grandma sent
her warmest love. I suppose John was about three at the time, and I can still
remember his bright eyes quizzing me as he looked expectantly and said,
'. . . and some chocolate?'

At his age, love could be better appreciated if it had some visible form.
Perhaps the world would be a better place if we learned to express our love
in acts, showing our feelings for one another a little more openly, giving
appreciation more often, adding a little 'chocolate' to our good wishes.

Along the Way

INHIBITED

THERE is so much locked away inside me, Master,
so much that no one else knows about but You;
>   my hopes, desires . . . and fears.
Why can't I open my heart to someone else
>   to get advice and counsel?
Why must I bar the door of my being to others,
>   keeping them out
so that I can hold myself intact within?

Am I afraid of others knowing how I am inside,
learning that I am not always what I seem to be?
Getting to know the real me, perhaps not at all as acceptable
>   as the visible image?
What a relief it would be, Lord,
>   to allow all defences to fall . . .
>   to talk without reservation
>   and without fear of misunderstanding
>   or harsh judgement.

Am I the only one who feels like this, Master?
Or are all people locked within their being,
>   never fully expressing themselves
>   because of a barrier of restraint
>   or a fear of ridicule?

How good it is that I can talk to You, Lord.
When I am alone I can even speak out loud,
>   putting into words to You
>   what I cannot tell others.
You are my safety valve, the patient Listener,
and at the same time Helper and Guide.
How could I live without You?

Towards You, Lord

FINGERTIPS

ALIVE to my fingertips, Lord!
>   What a glorious experience!
Thank You a thousand times for the sense of touch
bringing so much pleasure.
My fingers talk to me!

Through touch they give me all kinds of
      useful information:
      cold or heat, curves or angles,
the smoothness of silk and the roughness of sacking.

Yet think how I have used my fingers
      (and sometimes misused them!).
First the infant joy of sucking them,
then exploring with them, grabbing, tearing.
With them I have learned to write, sew, knit and type.
I have burnt my fingers on a hot stove
and frozen them while playing in the snow.
They have been recorded on my identity card
      in foreign lands,
a series of black smudges which by some
      strange alchemy
means that I am *me* and nobody else.

My fingertips are worn with housework
      and gardening,
flattened by the typing of thousands of pages,
yet they still report faithfully to me
the merest crack on a glass or cup
or the end of a roll of sticky tape.
The only thing I have not been able
      to train them to do
is to open cellophane packaging but
      fortunately there are scissors!
A huge thank You, Master, that I am still
      alive to my fingertips!

My God and I

10 AUGUST

FAULTY FINGERTIPS

MY prints were recorded for police annals in South America, on my identity card and records. I recall the incident very clearly for my fingerprints were reported as faulty and I had to blacken my fingers again on the pad provided and make fresh prints. Only then was it discovered that I had a scar on my left index finger. Well I know how it came there. At eight years of age I was going to show how clever I was by cutting the loaf and the knife slipped and gashed my finger. I have borne the scar throughout my life, but I am still alive to my fingertips!

Along the Way

11 AUGUST

REJECTION

MASTER, I feel worthless;
        unloved, unwanted, brushed aside,
        cheapened in my own eyes
        and in the view of others.

How much of the blame is mine?
        Some part, of course.
My tongue is too sharp and quick
        for the comfort of those around me;
my sulky moods depress and chill my environment,
my seeming arrogance is really only a veneer
        to cover inward insecurity.

Lord, I turn to You in desperate need.
I want to be accepted . . . and loved
        but I only meet with rejection.
Can You save me from myself?
Can You make me into a new person
        with different ways?
Can You break down the wall of my self-centredness
        and make a window out to others?

O God . . . I'm at the end of my tether!
You must help me for no one else can.
        I place myself in Your hands.
I ask You to forgive all my sins and failings.
Create in me a clean heart
        and let me make a new beginning,
looking up to You instead of inward to myself,
        and claiming Your aid.

Towards You, Lord

12 AUGUST

KNEES BEND

IN a television programme housewives were given the good advice to bend their knees when picking up things, instead of bending their backs. This could save a good deal of backache, and it is certainly more graceful.

Further tips were to alternate arms when pushing or pulling a carpet sweeper, shopping trolley or child's pram. It sounds just plain common sense and yet many of us get set in our pattern of movements as though we were machines monitored to a certain programme, instead of human beings with flexible muscles in a highly adaptable and ingenious body.

I once read the intriguing advice that to keep fit one should 'move everything that is movable' in the body each day. Unused muscles get weak and flaccid. Over-used muscles respond by aching. Share out the jobs to be done among all your muscles and they will respond with happy service.

Along the Way

THIS ONE DAY

THIS one day, Lord, is mine.
Your gift to me, fresh from Your hands;
      heralded by the twittering of birds,
      cleansed by the dawn wind,
      warmed by the sun's first rays . . .
This day is mine!

This one shining day is my own.
      I bless its early hours
      as I commit it to You.
I yield myself into Your care
knowing I am secure in Your love,
      whatever the coming hours may bring.

Please, Master, make it a good day,
      filled with happy work-hours
      and rewarding leisure,
a really-good-to-be-alive day.

Let today be a day I shall remember,
not because of some world-shaking event,
      but because it was a golden day,
      glowing with happiness.
Let it be a day of inward harmony and outward peace,
      of joybells within and laughter without;
a carefree rollicking kind of a day
when my heart spins its own thread of fun,
to weave a bright pattern through all that happens.

And when I lay my head on my pillow tonight,
let my heart be warm with gratitude to You
      for all life's good gifts.
Let my last thought be a contented:
      'Thank You, Lord.'

Towards You, Lord

147

BUTTONS

YOU spoke to me today, Master,
      as I did a very ordinary task.
I cut the buttons off a worn-out garment
      before consigning it to oblivion,
      or at least the indignity of the rag-bag.
As I added the buttons to the multitude in the box
      a vocal chorus reached my inner ear.
Do you remember me? From your old coat . . .
And me? From that blue dress you used to like.
And us? You bought us and never used us.

Memories . . . I was held by memories of garments that had been
      and occasions when I'd worn them;
some that I felt happy in, others that I never liked.
Looking in that old button-box
      was like wandering round a cemetery,
      reading well-known names on headstones.

No! that's not right! The buttons were not dead, only retired,
      and fully equal to a new emergence
      when the right time came.
I promised them I wouldn't forget them,
wouldn't buy new buttons without going first to the button-box,
to search for, and surely to find, just what I needed.

I fancied I heard a sigh of satisfaction, Lord,
as I closed the button-box lid.
Nothing and no one likes to be considered useless,
      and that includes people, of course.
That was probably the point I was being led to, Master.
Help me to make old people feel
      that they still have some purpose in life,
      still something to give that is of value.

Between You and Me, Lord

INSTANT EVERYTHING

MORE and more commodities are becoming 'instant', requiring only the addition of water or milk to make them ready for use. It is very tempting when one is in a hurry, and who isn't in these days?

    Some things, though, will never be 'instant'. There is no instant growth in either the natural or the spiritual world, there is no instant maturity, no instant saintliness, no instant dexterity. Many things in life can only be produced or won at slow tempo, with great patience and endurance.

One thing God does supply on the instant is forgiveness, his great loving heart blotting out our misdeeds and receiving us as his children.

Praise to his name for instant acceptance!

Along the Way

COOKING FOR ONE

IT'S pointless, Master, cooking for one!
All that time and trouble to end in sitting alone with a tray.
>It's tragi-comic . . .
One potato simmering in solitary seclusion,
two sausages huddled together for warmth
>in the centre of the frying pan,
>an apple for dessert.
I know I ought to be grateful to have the chance to
>prepare a meal, even a simple meal,
>while others go without,
but it does seem a waste of time and energy.

Of course, I could make cooking my dinner a hobby,
producing all kinds of delicious morsels to tempt my appetite,
but, Lord, I've noticed that I eat more when I'm alone.
It's a kind of compensation and it does make time pass.
>I can't afford to overeat,
not only from the money standpoint, but so as to fit my clothes
>which will have to serve me for a very long time.

Help me to be sensible about food, Lord.
>Let me take short, easy methods
yet get what my body needs to keep fit,
for You're counting on me for some involvement yet.
When my meal is ready, I'll turn on the radio or TV
>or else prop up a good book beside me.
Not always, though . . . Sometimes I'll recall what You said:
>'If any man opens the door, I'll come in
>and eat with him and he with Me.'
Help me to keep the door of my heart open to You, Lord,
>for You are the best of company
>and with You plain fare becomes a feast.

Between You and Me, Lord

ILL-TIMED PRAYERS

IT was my mistake, Lord.
I thought that event was today and found
    it took place yesterday.
There was I praying for Your blessing
    on a past happening . . .
What do You do with such ill-timed prayers?
I cannot think, Master, that they are simply cast
    into Your Heavenly waste-paper basket
    as useless lumber.
Surely in the divine economy
    You will be able to use them.

Do I imagine too much when I picture
    a Heavenly conveyor belt
    ceaselessly moving forward,
carrying prayers, longings, desires,
    from the past into the future?
Into that stream of directed power
    my simple prayer must have fallen;
not availing much for the particular moment
    I had in mind
but becoming a tiny drop in the strengthening
    stream of grace
    flowing before Your throne
    for re-channelling earthwards.

I'm not worried then, about my mistimed prayers,
You will use them somehow, somewhere, Lord.

God in My Everyday

MY FORGOTTEN BIRTHDAY

IT is not easy to be a stranger in a strange land, where you do not speak the language easily and are new to the customs and the climate. My mind goes back to our first months in Sweden. I had learnt a little Swedish but still felt strong attachment to my homeland, England, from which we had come. My husband had been sent as translator with a group to London so it was arranged for me with my two small sons to stay at The Salvation Army's holiday home outside Stockholm.

    Before he left my husband had given me a little gift for my birthday which would occur while he was travelling. I had made up my mind not to let anyone at the holiday home know it was my birthday and also not to feel too bad about the fact that I must spend it alone in a new land mostly among strangers. However, during the day a mood of depression crept over me and I was tempted to feel 'forgotten' for I had received no post.

I fought against the temptation to self-pity and tried to make the day a happy one for my little boys, but it was with rather a heavy heart that I went to bed that night. Next morning as I attended to my baby I heard singing outside the window. To my great surprise, in walked some of the people in the home with coffee and cakes and some small parcels for my birthday. I was utterly confounded when they said: 'Many happy returns of the day.' I thanked then warmly but gave no expression to the big question at the back of my mind. As soon as they had left me, I jumped out of bed and pulled out the small calendar from my handbag. It was my birthday! I had thought it was the day before and had not checked on the date seeing I was living in the country. That was a lesson to me!

I had thought I was forgotten. I had been tempted to wallow in self-pity. I had felt depressed and lonely. And all the time loving hearts were planning a happy surprise for me when the right time came.

Perhaps that is how the Lord treats us?

When we think we are forgotten he is planning some new token of his love and care. Can we not believe that?

Ur Minnets Gömmor (Down Memory Lane)

MY UNTENTED SOUL

WHEN I was a teenager I had a bad attack of influenza and imagined that I was dying. By my bedside I had a recently acquired volume of John Oxenham's poems and it occurred to me that I could leave a final message to the world in some of his lines.

I was deeply moved when I thought of how the finding of these lines, duly underscored, beside my dead body would affect the mourners. Then they would realise what a treasure had gone from their midst. The lines I left as my last message were these – as far as memory permits:

> *Fold up the tent.*
> *The sun is in the west,*
> *Tomorrow my untented soul*
> *Will roam among the blest;*
> *And I am well content,*
> *For rest is best.*

That was about 60 years ago and my soul is still 'tented'.

Along the Way

MINIATURE CHRISTIANS

MINIATURES are popular, Master,
particularly in the gardening world
but hardly, I think, in Your realm.
Dwarf plants are cultivated,
roots are severed, nourishment restrained,
anti-growth mixtures applied and for what?
To produce a miniature tree
to stand in a pot on the coffee table.

If You, Lord, are not eager for dwarf Christians,
the Evil One is intent on their propagation.
He encourages a little religion, an outward show,
oh! nothing extravagant of course,
just sufficient to produce a miniature Christian
with stunted growth,
no depth of root into Your truths,
merely a shallow show of outward conformity.

You want virile, dedicated, all-out followers,
trees of righteousness
standing strong, free and unbending
against evil attacks
or the dangerous drought of an indifferent world.

Drop Your spiritual fertilisers into our souls, Lord,
expanding the spread of our branches,
speeding our searching roots,
making us trees of the Lord, full of vitality,
living witnesses to Your power.

God in My Everyday

POSTAL GRILLING

RECENTLY I received a letter from a student, asking me all sorts of questions about myself as a writer. She intended to prepare a thesis about me and wanted to turn me inside out to find out what made me tick, what had started me off, what I was aiming at or hoping to achieve.

That certainly made me think.

It is good at times to sit down and evaluate one's own life and when questions are fired in swift succession from someone else's point of view new aspects can emerge and new ideas take form.

I did my best to satisfy the young lady and she promised to send me a copy of the result, which will certainly interest me.

Along the Way

AGGRIEVED

I'M feeling aggrieved, Lord, really put out,
      over a very small matter too.
I'm ashamed to admit, Master,
that it was just a change of TV programme
which no longer fitted my lunch hour.
I enjoyed watching and listening to it
      as I ate alone.
It was company, it gave interest
      and *it was part of my day.*

So I feel peeved and disappointed.
      I never realised before
how much I relied on that programme
      to accompany my meal.
I could of course postpone my lunch
      a couple of hours,
but that would upset the rhythm of my day.

Lord, at the same time that I am annoyed,
      I am appalled . . .
appalled that so small a thing as a change
      of programme
can upset me to such a degree,
while the world shudders and writhes in wars,
      earthquakes and bombings.
It is nonsense that I should feel so deprived –
a momentary weakness that I must overcome.
      You will help me, Lord?
      I know You will.

God in My Everyday

FAVOURITE TEXTS (1)

THE overabundance of translations makes it more difficult to memorise and retain texts nowadays, which in many ways is a pity, but the essential fact is that the truth of God's word penetrates and enlightens our mind whatever translation is used.

Along the Way

FAVOURITE TEXTS (2)

WE need a supply of texts in our minds that we can draw upon for all occasions, turning them over to extract every hidden shade of meaning. It is strange how God's Holy Spirit lights up a well-known text with new meaning just at the moment we need guidance or comfort.

Along the Way

25-30 AUGUST
From *My God and I* pages 45-54

THE PATH OF PRAYER

(1) LESSONS IN PRAYING

HOW shall I pray, Lord?
I remember Your short, pointed prayer
    beginning 'Our Father'.
I remember too Your nights of intense vigil
    on lonely mountain slopes;
Your early rising, withdrawing from company,
Your need to be alone with God.

    Teach me to pray, Master.
Not following Your pattern slavishly
but adapting it to my own circumstances,
to my family, my work and my needs.
I see that there must be times of united prayer
when with others I pray to *our* Father.
I must be part of a believing group of fellow Christians,
pouring out to You our corporate needs,
    our longings,
    our inadequacies,
    our cries for help, for forgiveness and peace.

But there must be times when I pray alone.
In those times I may not literally be by myself
    but one in a crowd;
a noisy happy crowd or a boring self-centred group.
Yet in my heart I can speak to You,
    knowing that You hear.
It may be only in bed at night or before I rise in the morning,
while waiting for bus or train or out shopping.
These moments with You can be my spiritual snacks
    along the way,
until such time as I can spend some quiet moments
    apart with You.

(2) TEPID PRAYERS

LORD, I am guilty! Guilty of tepid praying;
cool, casual, passionless prayers,
      just a formality.
      Forgive me!
I know that tepid prayers get nowhere.
They rise no higher than the ceiling,
      they accomplish nothing.

Many old-timers used to utter blazing prayers.
They were even called 'hot-gospellers'!
They clanged the bells of Heaven's gate
until they got their message through.
Has the heat gone out of all praying
      or only out of me?

Perhaps what we need, Master, is a new era,
      a rebirth of incendiary prayers
that will kindle a blaze in other hearts,
setting them afire for Your cause.
Desperate, persistent, believing prayers.
      Stir me up, Lord! Enthuse me, revitalise me,
until my tepid prayers come to the boil
and achieve some purpose according to Your will.

(3) CLUTTER

MY head, Lord, is filled with clutter.
      I want to pray,
      I intend to pray,
      I try to pray . . .
but the clutter vanquishes my good intentions.
      Silly little things,
      small irritations,
      plans for today, and tomorrow!
Thoughts whizzing round, chasing each other
      but never rising to You.
I make an effort, Master,
      I quote a text,
feed my mind on it for an instant
then the avalanche of trivia swallows it.
      I'm sorry, Lord.

I'll have to try again later.
I read a prayer or two with beautiful words.
They stir my mind but not my heart.

Yet I don't live a cluttered life.
My home is always reasonably tidy and
        any business attended to.
It is in my thoughts there is this muddle,
too many ideas chasing each other
        on a perpetual roundabout.
Is it a wile of the devil?
His way of getting between me and You?
        Sometimes I think it is.
At other times I blame myself for lack of concentration,
for want of purpose and of perseverance.
        Do help me, Lord!

28 AUGUST

(4) DIVINE PATIENCE

SOMETIMES I wonder, Lord, how You can
        endure man's follies . . .
defiant sinning, wilful choice of evil,
dishonesty, cruelty, intolerance, hate . . .
How can You look down upon us,
this world You have brought into being,
this humankind You have created,
        yet withhold Your hand
from smiting us to extinction
        by a passing meteor?
Your long-suffering is beyond belief,
Your love for us beyond all credence!
Your patient working out of a
        slowly evolving plan
is beyond the grasp of human understanding.

Yet when I look within my own heart
I see in microcosm the same defects . . .
potential marred by inadequacies
        or by deliberate wrongdoing.
In spite of that, Lord, You hold on
        to Your chosen course,
both for the world and the human heart.

156

You fulfil Your purpose slowly, oh! so slowly
with such divine tenderness and patience.
I am melted with wonder at Your love,
        humbled and grateful
yet exasperated at Your slow deliberate pace.
My expostulations will not alter that, I know,
so grant me, Master, if it is possible,
a tiny morsel of Your endless patience.

(5) IS *RADIO* TO BLAME?

LORD, is radio to blame or television perhaps
        for my inattention to prayer?
I am so used to having words poured into my ear
        from the mass media
that possibly I am losing the power
        to think for myself,
        to concentrate,
        to express what I feel.
Am I simply a sponge soaking up from others
        all the time?
Should my form of self-denial not be
        to shut off the media at times
        so as to think, really think,
        and *pray?*
I tried it this morning as I started my cleaning.
Instinctively my hand went out to touch
        the radio button.
Then I hesitated and decided to work in silence,
        lifting my heart to You,
        talking to You
instead of listening to a programme.

The name of a missionary came to my mind
so I prayed for her while I dusted.
        Did that help her?
        I can't prove that it did
but it drew me closer to her for a few moments.
Give me the courage, Master, the sheer grit
required to turn off the radio more often
and to face the ensuing silence . . . with You.

(6) A LONG WAY OFF

SOME words from Your Book came as balm
    to my spirit today, Lord.
In the parable of the prodigal son
    who decided to return home
    when money and friends had gone
it is recounted that while the lad was yet 'a long way off'
his father saw him and ran to meet him.

I am not a prodigal, Master, in the usual sense
but just a very feeble follower of Yours.
At times I realise that I am still 'a long way off'
yet my steps are turned towards You
though my progress is laborious.

Great comfort comes to me as I compare mentally
    the slow steps of the son
    and the eager pace of the father.
I believe it is a true picture of how You meet
    with us in prayer.
You come more than half-way towards us
and with an urge of self-giving love
    You seek to meet our needs.

Help me to keep that picture in my mind, Master,
    when prayer seems a dull duty
    rather than a privilege.
You are on Your way to meet me
even while I am procrastinating and still 'a long way off'.

POSTURE IN PRAYER

THE kneeling attitude in prayer seems to be less and less adopted. It is certainly not comfortable to hold for any long time. I well remember when I was a cadet 60 years ago (!) how we used to sink to our knees in the street during an open-air meeting, our thoughts inevitably fixed on the effect it would have on our long skirts.

The other day I noticed a very relaxed prayer attitude of an old patriarch in the Bible. 'Jacob, just before he died, leaned on the top of his walking-stick and worshipped God' (Hebrews 11:21, *Good News Bible*).

Along the Way

MY ENEMY

MASTER, You said some hard things.
You said: 'Love your enemies.'
At first sight it does not look so difficult,
as long as I think of my enemies as out there, far, far away.
In jungles where matted grasses block the paths,
in hot, barren deserts where goat-skin tents sprawl like
          overgrown mushrooms close to the baked ground,
in the cold north and south lands where they fight blizzards
          through the long, dark winters;
in great noisy cities where they drive their cars on the
          wrong side of the road.

Enemies?
They are people with features other than my own,
          neither better nor worse, just otherwise.
They are people with skins unlike my own,
          neither better nor worse, just different.
They are people with languages I can't understand,
          strange to my ears.
Those imaginary enemies that I shall never see or know,
          those I can think kindly of,
          those I can pray for,
          those I can love.

But, Lord, it is my enemy next door that troubles me.
Her children pick my flowers,
her dog dirties my front path,
her drab washing flaps uglily when I have visitors;
she is not tidy in her dress and sometimes – this is just
          between You and me, Lord – she smells.
Lord, do You really expect me to love *her*?
I'm quite prepared to go halfway,
          to come to some arrangement with her,
          so that we can co-exist in a state of armed neutrality over
          the garden fence.

But *love* her? Lord, You ask the impossible.
          I can't do it.
Will You help me by showing me how to achieve the
          impossible?

                              Just a Moment, Lord

THE UNWANTED GIFT

IT is some time since it happened, Lord,
      but it still smarts a bit.
      My gift was unwelcome.
Oh! it was quite a simple thing
but it had cost me some time to make
and I had hoped it would give pleasure.
Much later I found it put away in a cupboard,
      unused and unwanted.

My immediate reaction was to feel hurt.
Some of myself had gone into my gift.
Master, I began to feel badly disappointed,
      then suddenly I saw reason.
I had given my friend what I thought she would like
      without checking with her beforehand.
I had enjoyed planning and making it
      according to my own ideas
and naively expected her to be delighted.
I wanted both the pleasure of giving a gift
but also of being thanked and praised.

Sometimes, Lord, I wonder how You feel
      about our offerings to You.
We give a little time, money, service,
      feeling how generous we are
      and how pleased You must be.
Do You ever reject our gifts? I don't think so;
I believe You accept them warmly,
magnanimously overlooking their insignificance,
like a good father with his child.

God in My Everyday

BARGAINING

MASTER, forgive me my bargaining prayers!
      I am ashamed of them.
'If You grant my request then I promise . . . '
What I ask and what I promise hardly matters
for the whole idea is wrong
and within me I know that full well.
      You and I know, Lord,

that when the request is granted
the promise is often forgotten.

You are not the free supplier of a coloured catalogue
        of valuable items I might need
        and certainly want,
which I can obtain simply by applying at no cost to myself.

Your purpose is not to supply every whim
        of a spoilt child
nor provide for an adult's passing fancy.
You do not require me to tell You my needs
        for You know me too well.
Help me to leave the issue with You,
simply yielding myself into Your hands:
        leaving my future with You,
        concentrating on today alone
and asking that I may know and do Your will.
What You grant me daily of grace and mercy
far exceeds anything I might deserve.
        Let me be grateful,
        truly grateful.
Let me cease trying to bargain with You.

My God and I

4 SEPTEMBER

EVERYDAY COURAGE

FROM Leslie Weatherhead's *A Private House of Prayer* I cite these meaningful words:

'May we never sell our courage to buy sympathy. Show us that silent suffering, without bitterness or self-pity, can make us strong.

From advertising our self-martyrdoms, from blazing abroad our little sacrifices, from reciting our woes to others, O Lord, deliver us.

Enrich our lives, we beseech Thee, with those experiences which seem most hard to bear. May we be more ready to give to others our bread and our wine, than to tell them of our hunger and our thirst.'

Along the Way

5 SEPTEMBER

A FAVOURITE MAXIM

FROM a fellow septuagenarian who follows a strict health food diet, and is herself full of boundless energy, I give you the following:

'If you take care of your inside the outside will take care of itself.'

Along the Way

EMPTY!

FOLK said it was a good talk, Master;
thoughts running freely, words chosen with care,
but as I took my seat I heard Your silent verdict:
>'Empty!'

I don't want to be an empty can, Lord.
I don't want to be a showcase filled with duds.
>I want to be real, through and through;
not only real myself, but filled with Your presence,
>transmitting Your love and Your life.

Oh frightening emptiness . . .
>a hollow soul,
>just a shell!
>Save me from that, Master.

Of course it might have been the Tempter's whisper.
He's always trying to spike my guns,
to destroy my defences from within,
>old Quisling that he is.
You must forgive me, Lord, if I say that I can hardly tell
>the difference between Your voice and his.
He's a master hand at imitation.
If I could be sure it was him talking I wouldn't care.
But I have a feeling, a strong feeling, that it was You.
And before the verdict from Your lips of 'Empty!' I quail.

>I don't want to be a vacuum, Master!
>Fill me, fill me with Your Spirit
>so that I have something to give,
>something direct from You –
>a live transmission.

Just a Moment, Lord

'WOMEN I DISLIKE'

AMONG my papers I found a scrap torn from a pad and marked: 'Home League'. It was a draft for a talk which, fortunately, I never gave, with the title: 'Women I dislike'. By the yellowing of the paper I know the notes are of ancient vintage although – unlike wine – they have probably not improved with keeping. I hardly dare to give you my main points:

1. Models of housewifely virtue, who always have their homes spick and span, their children immaculate, husbands well fed and content, yet have time to sew, paint, garden, chat, etc, etc.

2. Curious women, who ask intimate questions about family, friends, plans, relations, the price of your dress, where you bought it, what you paid for your Sunday joint, why you do this or that, etc.

3. The inveterate borrower, always coming to your door and never returning the shears, bag of sugar, recipe, book or steam iron.

4. The whiner – her ailments, details of operations, troubles, problems, setbacks.

5. The self-absorbed – her house, children, work, views, flowers she likes and dislikes, the books she has read, holidays she has had and the people she knows.

What a good thing I never gave that talk! I can imagine that by the time I had finished my audience would have disappeared, fearing that I was going to round upon them all. The only saving feature of those old-time notes is the quote at the end which says:

'If each before his own door swept, the village would be clean.'

I hope I was going to make a suitably humble admission of my own shortcomings.

Along the Way

8 September

DOORSTEP SURPRISE

THE doorbell rang as I was having my tea. Answering it I found a small round-faced girl, about eight years old, clutching a list and a collecting box. She seemed discomfited to see me, even slightly startled.

Then she re-collected herself, smiled and said, 'Hallo'.

I replied in like manner.

By the expression on her face I could see that she was doing some rapid thinking, then her face cleared as she came to a decision. 'You're a poor old lady, aren't you?' she asked, not in the form of interrogation but rather as a sympathetic statement of fact.

Rather taken aback I answered, 'Well, I'm old, but I'm not particularly poor.'

'Never mind,' she replied, 'Cheerio! Goodbye!' and with a smile she tripped down the garden path to the gate. I suppose she was collecting for 'poor old ladies' and felt she couldn't, or shouldn't, appeal to me.

Along the Way

GLUTTONY

GLUTTONY, Lord, is an ugly word,
        and it conjures up a bad image
of a fatty brandishing knife and fork
and gourmandising from heaped-up dishes.
Your Book reminds us that gluttony
        is one of the seven deadly sins,
but we hear very little about it otherwise.

You, Master, were called 'a glutton
        and a wine-bibber'.

That gives me something to think about.
        No one can escape
the poisoned barbs of criticism,
but they wing their way with deadlier aim
        tipped with a snippet of truth.
It is recorded that You graced many
        a laden table with Your presence.
You enjoyed festivities and special occasions,
and You certainly did not frown on them.

Yet Your everyday life was uncluttered and simple,
        as befitted a wandering Teacher.
At Your death Your only possession of value
        was a seamless tunic –
no doubt a gift, not a purchase.
Master, from You I must learn the delicate balance
between personal austerity and rejoicing with others
        at festive moments.
Even so, guard me from self-indulgence
        and the sin of gluttony.

God in My Everyday

WORDS TO PONDER

'YOU who are saying that your religion does not save you from sorrow and suffering, nor dry your tears, nor mend your broken hearts; remember that I do not think it was ever meant to.

'It was meant to give you power rather than satisfaction; hope rather than happiness; courage to face sorrow rather than safeguards against it.'

From a sermon by Dick Sheppard.
Along the Way

POOR OLD SOUL

I USED to say that myself, Master,
when in my bumptious youth I thought
that anyone over thirty was finished, *out* . . .
and that at forty one had a foot in the grave;
yet here I am at the three-score-year-and-ten mark,
still apparently going strong
and quite happy to be old.

I wouldn't want to live my life over again, Lord.
There have been too many painful passages,
too many struggles,
too many disappointments . . .
I feel like a ship that is entering a long-sought harbour,
storm-worn, with sun-blistered paint
yet chugging along on the old faithful engine
towards a final docking.

Youngsters now think of me as a 'poor old soul'!
They can save their pity for I need none.
I like being old,
I enjoy being old.
The questings and questionings are mostly behind me;
my expectations are modest so there are less disillusions,
my wants are not many,
my needs even fewer.
In Your goodness You have granted me a kind of wisdom
so that my reaction to unpleasant news is not as violent,
my judgements not so harsh.
This mellowing is one of the bonuses of growing old
for which I thank You, Lord.

So this 'poor old soul' is a happy and fulfilled old soul.
Thank You, Master, for Your great part in that.
With You I can make the last bit of the way.

Between You and Me, Lord

NEVER PUT THINGS AWAY

I SAY this to myself in exasperation many times after a clearing-up!
Beforehand I knew where papers, letters and other items were; once I have tidied up and put them out of sight I can never find them again.

Along the Way

PRICE TAB

IT gave me a real start, Master,
to see myself suddenly in the mirror
with a price tab hung round my neck.
Had I been walking round like that all morning?
      Shopping, chatting, bus-queueing
      with a white price ticket
dangling for all to see?

I moved and my reflection in the shop window moved.
      With a great sigh of relief
I realised that the price tab was left behind
      hanging on a wax model.
It was *her* price, not mine
      that was displayed.

It had given me a momentary shock, Master,
so unpleasant that I had not read
      the figure on the ticket.
What did *she* cost? What was *I* worth?
That question followed me all day.
If we all wore realistic price tabs of our worth
in terms of what we contribute to life,
      what eye-openers there would be!
Some very ordinary people would be highly priced,
while front-line figures might be half-price bargains.

What a good thing that we are not asked
      to set a price upon ourselves,
      or more to the point, on others.
Only You, Master, know our true worth
      and judge us accordingly.

God in My Everyday

THE PENALTIES OF GROWING OLD

ONE of the penalties of growing old is that the corners of one's mouth begin
to droop in repose, giving a depressed, even an unhappy look, to a normally
quite cheerful person. But what a miracle occurs when that person smiles!
Suddenly the face is illumined, transformed, radiant . . .
    What a pity we can't go around in a state of continual delight!

Along the Way

BRINGING UP GRANDMA

MY Danish grandson Alan is a kind little gentleman, and in a friendly way he gave me some very good counsel. I had put the kettle on for tea without noticing which way the spout pointed. Alan, helping to lay the table, said: 'Grandma, the kettle spout shouldn't face the wall as some of the steam might make the wallpaper damp.'

I thanked him with due humility and rectified my mistake.

Along the Way

A GUTTERING CANDLE

A GUTTERING candle is no pleasant sight.
Had it tongue to speak, what might it say?

Look not on what I am now,
        but what I was.
        Tall, straight, shapely.
Bravely I shed my light on all around,
knowing that as I gave, I was myself consumed.

Harsh winds of life beat upon me,
        challenging my right to shine,
        fluttering my flame hither and thither.
        My strength dripped from me,
        yet I remained alight,
        faintly flickering.

Lord, this guttering candle speaks to me.
I, too, have known the pride of youth and strength,
held my head high and daily done my tasks.

But now the sun has passed its zenith,
strain and stress of duties have taken their toll,
winds of change have whirled around me,
        but, by Your grace,
        my light still burns.
Grant me one favour, Master.
Let my light flicker until the end,
until my flame sinks spent
        into final rest.

Just a Moment, Lord

I DON'T LIKE DRAINS

I DON'T like drains,
but it was humiliating for me to be
reproved by a neighbour
over what was apparently *my* dirty drain.
It was my first experience, Lord, of living
in an upstairs flat,
and I was newly married, quite unused
to managing a home.
It never occurred to me that it was my responsibility
to clean the garden drain.
I had never given a moment's thought
to where our bath water went!
The downstairs neighbour's sneering remark
came as a great surprise,
but having learnt my duty in that painful way
I performed the unpleasant task.

I am a Christian, Lord, one of Your followers,
and I knew I should have to do something,
some kind little act
to kill my resentment against that woman.
Is it swanking, Master, to tell You how?
When she was ill I cleaned her step
for a whole week.
Down on my knees with the scouring stone in my hand
(for that was the era we lived in then!)
I prayed that my voluntary penance might heal
the breach between us.
I'm glad to report that she thawed towards me
over the months,
though we never became real friends.

My God and I

DOWN THE DRAIN

WITHOUT drains we should, very unfortunately, find ourselves back in the 'good old days' when refuse was thrown from the window into the street. That life runs smoothly in the drain and sewer departments is due to the unseen functioning of much that we take for granted. What brought the subject of drains to my mind was the memory of a visit that my sister and I paid to the extensive sewers under Paris. We did it more as a joke than a serious study, but we have never regretted it. We had seen sewer visits listed among the tourist attractions in Paris. And it was free!

At the time appointed we met with other interested people in the splendid Place de la Concorde and, suppressing inward giggles, we climbed through a manhole in the pavement, down a series of steps and took our places in a flat-bottomed boat floating on dark waters in a tunnel lit by electric light. Two men, one on each side, pulled our boat along. Everything was most clean and hygienic, and there was no bad smell.

The walls of the tunnel were covered with numerous cables which we were told were for telephone, telegraph and pneumatic telegraph (by which express letters in Paris were suctioned along for rapid delivery). Our boat ride lasted only 10 minutes, then we were asked to alight. We climbed up some narrow stairs and emerged rather shamefacedly through a manhole in the pavement right in front of the stately Madeleine Church.

Our faces were red with hidden laughter as we tried to mingle nonchalantly with the passing crowds, pretending that we had not just come out of a drain.

Along the Way

19 SEPTEMBER

HE LOST HIS HEAD

TRANSLATORS, especially those who skilfully turn one language into another at the speed of sound, have my deepest admiration. It is not so boring as might be imagined to listen when you know both the languages used. To be able to admire the clever turn of phrase or, at times, suppress hidden mirth when the translator misses the meaning or changes a vital word defies boredom.

Once, in Copenhagen, during a congress meeting, the visiting officer used an illustration from a battlefield where a young soldier came under heavy fire. 'He lost his head,' she stated (having been advised to use short phrases) and that was translated. Then she continued with 'jumped out of the trench and ran.' There was dead silence from the translator for a moment then she turned to the speaker and said: 'He couldn't run; he was dead.'

The speaker insisted that the soldier wasn't dead; he had only 'lost his head' which from the translator's mouth, had become: 'His head was shot off' – a very reasonable assumption from someone knowing only acquired English. However, after heated discussion between the two ladies in the centre of the platform and an explanation to the audience, the address continued despite a certain hilarity in the hall.

Along the Way

FIRST THINGS FIRST

ON waking I lifted my heart to You, Master,
commending myself and my dear ones to Your care,
  even before I left the comfort of the warm bed.
I promised myself – and You –
that I would set aside a time for meditation and prayer
  as soon as breakfast was over.

With that intent I took Your Living Word downstairs
  with me to have it handy.
But other matters began to demand attention
  in domineering tones:
  The kitchen had to be cleared up
  and the front step washed
  (just in case anyone should call).
The cut flowers begged for fresh water . . . and got it
  and the duty treadmill span faster.

All the while I was conscious of Your gentle tapping
  at my heart's door and I whispered: 'I'll be ready soon.'
Finally the most urgent jobs were done
and I had just settled down to read Your Book
  when the telephone rang
with an urgent message calling for swift action.
  Then it was time for lunch.

I felt ashamed, Lord, really and truly ashamed.
I needed the renewal and refreshment of a time with You.
I hadn't robbed You so much as robbed myself
  of something vital and necessary.
Forgive me my weak will, Master, my succumbing
  to the temptation to put off doing first things first.
           Between You and Me, Lord

THE GIANT SPIDER WEB

A SPIDER has spun a huge web across one of my window panes. It was fascinating to have a front stall seat from which to watch his activity without him being aware of my presence on the inside of the pane.

How did he get that web to adhere far down the other side? I never saw him do it – he probably rises earlier than I do – but I imagine he waited for a gust of wind and then swung wherever it took him.

What faith in the spider's tiny mind; what strength in his instinct, that said: 'Launch out.' May we be as bold!

Along the Way

CURTAINS

I WALK the streets, Lord, and I see curtains at every window.
Some gay and fresh, others sallow and dusty and drab,
>> but nevertheless curtains.
I go home to my own curtained windows
>> and I ask myself why, Master.
Why do I, why do others,
>> keep windows draped with curtains?

Is it to shut ourselves in or others out
>> or a mixture of both?
Perhaps to give a chance of peeping out
>> without being seen?
There is something secretive about heavily curtained windows,
>> a kind of 'it's none of your business' attitude.
How far is that legitimate privacy
>> and how far is it selfish seclusion?

I remember the young couple whose business went bankrupt.
Little by little they sold all their belongings
>> but they kept the curtains at the windows
so that no one knew they were lying on bare boards
>> and eating standing at the kitchen sink.
There was something of tough heroism in that.
>> I could not blame them.

Curtains can hide a lot, Master,
hide it from prying gaze or from friendly glance,
>> but not from Your eyes . . .

You see it all! There is no possible cover-up with You
>> and I am glad it is so.
Some people curtain their souls against Your advance,
>> not daring to let You in.
Help me to open the windows of my inward being to You,
>> inviting You in with all You have to give me,
for You do not come to inspect but to encourage,
>> to share fellowship and impart strength.

Between You and Me, Lord

OLD PHOTOS

GHOSTS! Master,
   I've been seeing ghosts,
the shadowy phantoms of long ago.
Those who once were and now are not;
those who once were,
and are now so changed as to be unrecognisable.
Such gawky innocence! Such smooth-faced complacence!
   Was I really like that?
Those around me that I called friends,
   I recall them one by one.
What happened to break the warm bonds between us?
Nothing really. We just drifted apart,
our ways diverged and we formed new links.

In turning back the pages of my life, Lord,
I realise afresh Your goodness to me.
So much could have gone wrong that I was spared.
My very inexperience could have led to disaster,
   but You helped me to find a right solution.
As I regard the past, my heart praises You.

Through the photos the generations pass in cavalcade.
   The child becomes the parent
   and then the grandparent.
The smooth face becomes wrinkled, the straight form bowed,
   everything changes!
Then how good to know, Lord, that You remain the same,
   unchangeable in Your being,
   constant in Your loving care.

The old photos slip from my hands, Master.
   I leave them in the past
and I step out into the future with You beside me.
         Between You and Me, Lord

A GOOD CONSCIENCE

WHILE reading one of Solzhenitsyn's short stories I came across this delightful comment:
  'People who are at ease with their consciences always look happy!'
         Along the Way

A THOUGHT FROM F. B. MEYER

'IF this day I should get lost amid the perplexities of life and the rush of many duties, do thou search me out, gracious Lord, and bring me back into the quiet of Thy presence'.

Along the Way

From *Towards You, Lord* pages 101-107

BEREFT

IT'S happened to me, Master,
that heaviest blow to a marriage,
  the death of the beloved partner.
When we made our lifelong vows we knew it was
  'till death us part',
but that moment seemed aeons away in a misty future.
Now my turn has come to walk alone.
  I'm glad my loved one went first,
glad that I could tend and serve him to his last day.
  Thank You, Lord, for that.

Now I'm one of the great host of those who face single
   life
  after years of intimate comradeship.
I accept my lot without complaint
  for I am but one among many.
I have loved and been loved,
now I must meet life's challenges alone.

Master, it is not easy!
There is a painful shrinking from assuming burdens,
a desperate need to confide in someone,
  to share with another.
For a time it seems a half-life,
  a mechanical doing of duties,
  a painful remembering,
but Your presence relieves some of the sting
and gives hope for the days ahead.

One day there will be a reunion in that Beyond
  which You have prepared.
So help me, Lord, to live worthily,
making of each day something of value.

(2) HEARTACHE

HEARTACHE is a very real thing, Master,
a continuous pressure on the emotions
      that leaves one drained and weary.
Physical pain would be easier to bear
      for some remedy could be applied,
but this gnawing at the vitals of one's being
      knows no alleviation.

This inward hurting is hard to endure.
      Part of me has been wrenched away
and the wound is open, gaping open, Master,
yet I must hide it from others' eyes,
      for they would not understand.
Folk are kind to me and thoughtful, Lord, and I am grateful.
They remind me of all life still holds for me.
      I know their words are true
yet there is a revulsion of feeling within me
as though I must refuse to be comforted,
      at any rate for the time being.

Does time heal, Master? It is said that it does
      and I expect it is true,
but I crave more than that thought just now.
I want to feel Your loving arms around me,
I want to hear You say: 'Be comforted.
      Your loved one is with me.'
The warmth of Your presence will bring soothing balm.
Your loving care will wrap a tender mantle around me
      until my wounds are healed
      and my heartache assuaged.
Come to me just now, my Lord.

(3) STABS OF REMEMBRANCE

IT'S the little things, Master, that hurt most.
Stabs of remembrance pierce my heart
      over such tiny trifles,
      linked with a loved one
gone on the long journey from which no one returns.
That link gives them power to move me deeply.

An empty armchair shouts its disuse,
a well-worn purse brings a lump to my throat,
    a marking in a favourite book,
    an underlined text in the Bible
    or a cross against a chosen hymn,
all speak in potent language to my sensitive heart.

These swift stabs of remembrance bring pain, Lord,
    yet thankful, grateful pain,
    happy memories misted with sorrow,
a veil of regret thin enough to allow some of the light
    to shine through,
stings of memory glowing with warm feeling.
For these things only hurt because a love-relationship
    has been broken,
otherwise I should be indifferent to them.

It is the price of loving, to open one's heart to suffering.
As it is I can thank You for the memories they conjure up,
the rewarding companionship over the years,
    the living and doing,
    laughing and sorrowing, *together.*
The outer bond has snapped but the inner union remains,
    fanned into even brighter glow.
Praise God for memories, even if they sear with sudden pain.

(4) THE CUPBOARD IS BARE

MASTER, I know I shall need a lot for the days ahead:
    courage, patience, health and much more.
As I look over my spiritual shelves
    in an appraising stocktaking,
I find the cupboard is almost bare.

How can I face the lonely days, the fearful vista of time ahead,
dwindling to a misty nothingness where even my fertile
        imagination
fails to bring any clear and comforting contours?
My stock of inward resources for the future is nil,
    my cupboard is bare
and my heart feels frozen and frightened.

Then You speak to me, Lord. You say:
'It has never been My plan to provide grace in advance of need.

As you meet each new circumstance,
        I shall be there, giving you what you require.
Your cupboard will *always be empty,* but My resources
                are infinite
and in the moment of need I shall respond.
Call upon Me and I shall not fail you.'

So I live with my empty cupboard.
Its shelves will always be bare of spiritual stores,
but to my breast I clutch the promise of my God,
to fulfil all my needs in Christ, as they arise.

30 September

(5) MODERATION

LET me live with restraint, Lord,
reminding myself often that 'enough is enough.'
        This is good for me
for a measure of self-discipline will strengthen me.
It is so easy when one lives alone
to indulge in small luxuries;
to overeat, or oversleep, or over-rest.
After all, there is no one to criticise,
no one to praise or blame, indeed no one to see, so why not?

There is a reason, Master.
The spirit must remain in charge, in authority,
        or the body will take over,
        whimpering its needs and wants,
querulously demanding cosseting, craving to be pampered,
drowning out the voice of reason and restraint.

Quicken my conscience, Lord, without making it
        a hard taskmaster!
After all, I have to live with it,
so I can't afford to alienate it.
Let me use moderation not as a straitjacket,
        hampering and frustrating my movements,
but as a support, a standard, an ideal
which will lift my life above the merely material
and give me the stimulus of feeling that I am
        master over myself.
Let me repeat to myself daily that 'enough is enough'.

HELPS FOR THE SPIRITUALLY HANDICAPPED
(1) HEARING AIDS

SOMETIMES people say:
'God spoke to me and told me . . .'
Lord God, You have never spoken to me
in words, in actual words.
And yet I feel I have received Your guidance
by pressure on my spirit,
an insistence in my thoughts
or an opening up of unexpected paths.

In Your Book we read:
'The word of the Lord came to . . .'
Why then and not now?
Are we duller of hearing in our days?
Are we deafened by talk or music
whether from TV or radio, traffic or industry?
You speak to the inner ear, to the spirit.
Not even a clap of thunder could deaden Your voice.

It is we who are hard of hearing.
We need a spiritual hearing aid,
a means of greater receptivity such as
an awakened ear,
a *listening* ear.

There is the rub, Lord, I am sure.
We are not listening for Your voice
and therefore we do not hear it.
Help me to turn a listening ear towards You,
like the giant satellite dish tuning in
to the rhythm of the universe.
Speak to me, Lord!
And quicken my spiritual hearing
so that I can catch Your message.

2 OCTOBER

(2) SPECTACLES

HOW often, Lord, have I needed to confess to You
my spiritual short-sightedness!
My lack of vision of what You can do
with a surrendered life;

my failure to grasp what great resources are
        available to me
if I will but trust You and claim them
        for my own.

I see the world around me all too clearly!
        Its evil, its hates, its wars.
My own circumstances rise like a barrier,
        an immense, enclosing barrier,
shutting me in and You out.
I can't see any solution to my problems
        and my courage evaporates,
        my faith fails and I become spiritually blind.

Lord, open my eyes that I may see
        with spiritual vision, clear and true.
Let increased faith in You become for me
        a pair of spiritual spectacles,
compensating for my inadequate vision,
easing the strain of my struggles,
granting me a better perspective,
        a balanced view.
Grant me a vision of the world
        that includes You, that reckons with You
and rests upon the knowledge of Your might.

3 OCTOBER

(3) TELEPHONE

THEY were uneasy days, Master,
when my telephone was out of order.
Imagination ran rife as to what was happening
        to my dear ones
and why the post brought no letter.
For the elderly and housebound the telephone
        is a necessary lifeline
and its absence a severe trial.

Those days of deprivation taught me, Lord,
        how fortunate I am
to have a prayer-line to You at any hour
        night and day.
I can lift my heart to You with my need
        or just my grateful thanks
for all Your goodness, Your unending mercy.

178

I must confess I often make brief calls to You!
    Arrow prayers, short and direct,
which I believe wing their way Heavenward swiftly
and keep open my prayer-line to You.
How comforting to have someone always there,
        always ready to listen
        and full of living concern!

My telephone cable to Heaven never breaks down,
never gets enmeshed with other people's lines
so that I hear part of their monologue
        and they of mine!
That would be very embarrassing!
In addition, Master, the charges are always reversed
for no account ever comes from You,
nor do I have to pay a standing charge
        for my privilege.
Thank You, Lord . . . a big thank You!

(4) CRUTCHES

LORD, I need something to support me
for I am not a self-sufficient Christian,
able to shoulder each day's burden
        cheerfully,
and meet each new demand and challenge.
I need propping up and encouraging.
It is useless for me to pretend to be the
        strong, self-confident type,
sure of my faith and my God.
There are too many hesitations within me.
I can't step out bravely, helping others
        along the way.

It's I who need help, Lord! I need
        something to lean on, spiritual crutches.
With faltering faith came the feeble knees,
        the tottering gait
        and frequent stumbles.
I searched and found some spiritual crutches
        in the words of Your Book,
which speaks of strength being made perfect
        in weakness.

The promises are scattered like jewels through the pages,
each one something that I can cling to,
      lean on, claim as my own.

Slow I may be, Master, but I *am*
      making progress
though only one halting step at a time.
You will not fail me, Lord! I trust in You.

5 OCTOBER

(5) THE WALKING FRAME

I'VE seen people using them, Lord,
and my heart has felt compassion.
Recent invalids venturing out for a
      short, effortsome walk,
using the metal frame as a support.
I've seen them in hospital corridors,
trying out their legs after an operation
with so much effort, yet so much courage.
At times I feel I need a spiritual walking frame,
a constant support for every step I take
      along my pilgrim path.

Then it dawns upon me, Master . . .
I have a useful functional walking frame
      in my local church.
Bonded to fellow Christians I can move forward,
      aided by their faith and prayers.
Perhaps in time I can help someone else
      who is faltering,
      dispirited,
finding the going hard and lonesome.

Then a few chosen friends can be
      my strength and stay.
      I am not alone!
That thought enables me to look more hopefully
      to the days ahead.
I remind myself too of the Paraclete,
      the Holy Spirit,
the One sent alongside to help.
Thank You, Lord! I dare to claim Your strength
      for my weakness,
Your love for my every need.

(6) DOUBLE GLAZING

DOUBLE glazing is in fashion!
It is a practical way of shutting out cold,
        conserving indoor heat
and muffling street noises to a minimum.
Surely the Christian's soul needs double glazing too –
        against the chill of unbelief,
        the noise of selfish pursuits,
        the temptation to lower standards,
to watch in the shelter of home such films
as one would be ashamed to see in public?

God help us! We are beset on every hand!
        Our faith is attacked, our morals challenged
and the gospel message is ignored as obsolete,
        not for our times.

You did not pray, Master,
that we should be taken out of the world,
but that we should be kept from evil.
We must live in this modern generation
        with its joys and sorrows,
        its achievements and betrayals,
its flashes of goodness and surges of madness.
Be our guard against evil! Buttress us
        against its onslaughts,
be as double glazing to our souls,
protecting us from much that would besmirch,
keeping us safe in Your presence and
        conscious of Your nearness.
For this we pray, dear Lord.

(7) VITAMINS

WE all need them, Master, to keep ourselves healthy,
to increase our vitality and physical fitness.
But there are also vitamins of the spirit
        which we neglect at our peril,
        risking the loss of soul-strength.
These vitamins are hidden in Your Book, Lord,
        but are easy to find, simple to remember
and brief enough to learn by heart and carry

with us everywhere.
They are the great texts of the Bible,
assuring us of God's loving care,
of his plan and purpose,
confirming our faith
in the gospel message of forgiveness and redemption.

Spiritual vitamins are also found in good books
and films
whose challenges draw out the best in us;
which help to straighten our shoulders
under the daily burden of duties
and to give us a fresh infusion of courage.

Our friends, too, add the spice of fellowship
to the everyday,
revitalising us in many small ways.
For all these spiritual vitamins along the Christian pathway
we thank and praise You, Lord.

8 OCTOBER

(8) WHEELCHAIR

LORD, is a wheelchair a prison
or a platform?
Is it a punishment or a privilege?
Ask the handicapped and most reactions
will be positive:
'It gets me around and out and about!
What should I do without it?'

Many noble souls are tied to a wheelchair.
No! not tied, but users of one
as an instrument can be used in a band or orchestra,
contributing to life instead of being
dependent on others.
St Peter's 'wheelchair' was a prison cell
where he was double-chained to two soldiers.
That certainly restricted his movements!
The prophet Elijah had a special 'wheelchair'
provided for him by God
at the end of his life.
A chariot of fire pulled by fiery horses
took him to Heaven in a whirlwind.

None of us is likely to have such a
dramatic finish!

Lord, today I ask for Your blessing
on all in wheelchairs, young and old.
Grant them the grace of acceptance
        of the inevitable
but with it a real sense of Your presence
which will warm and cheer their hearts.

(9) ELDERLY LOOKALIKES

MASTER, we the elderly all look alike!
Some of us are a bit overweight and others
        rather skinny
but with the years, Lord, we become similar.
        Wrinkles, drab complexion, thinning hair,
        drooping mouth in repose,
        fumbling fingers and creaking joints
        plus perchance a walking stick.
But see us when we talk! We come alive!
Our eyes take on a cheerful shine
and smiles turn up the corners of the mouth,
smoothing out the ugly side lines.
The personality breaks out and
        age is forgotten!

If only we could grow old colourfully
        like autumn leaves!
Gorgeous rusty tints in our hair,
brilliant scarlet on our lips and cheeks . . .
Of course the cosmetic counter could supply
        all that for cash
but wouldn't it be nice, Master,
        if it were natural?
Away with these vain fancies!
Old age has to be faced and lived with
        as cheerfully as possible.
One thing is certain, Lord.
        We do not look alike to You!
You know us each as an individual.
You call us each by name.
        Thank You, Father.

183

FORGETTING

SOMETIMES, Lord, I forget.
      It is both annoying and unnerving.
At times I can laugh at myself,
      like when I go upstairs for a towel
      and bring down a book,
but at other times I feel scared, Master.
I find myself standing in front of an open cupboard
having completely forgotten what I came to fetch.
      It's not pleasant, Master,
      that side of ageing.
Of course part of the trouble is lack of concentration.
      I'm thinking of other matters.
Thank You for reminding me of that fact
      which brings me some comfort
      as well as a needed rebuke.

There is one thought that consoles me.
      I cling to Your promise, Lord,
      that You will never forget me.
If my memory should worsen
      so that like a shattered pot
      it holds nothing at all,
yet I am secure in Your hands,
      Your loving care surrounding me.

So I'll try to live with my forgetting
      without worrying too much about it.
By faith I claim Your strong Father-arms about me
      and I shelter snugly there.

Between You and Me, Lord

RIGHT AS RAIN

WHOEVER coined the phrase 'as right as rain?' When is rain *right*?

I know many occasions when it is wrong, when it interferes with plans and blocks pleasures. Could it be that the phrase originated in a desert land, when each drop of rain fell like blessing to a thirsty earth?

But why do we continue to use it, when we more often blame rain as a troublemaker than bless it for being just what we need?

Along the Way

GRACE BEFORE BREAKFAST

WHEN turning over some old newspaper cuttings I found the following:

'Lord, make us less like porridge, stodgy and difficult to stir; and more like corn flakes: crisp and ready to serve.'

And to that I say, Amen.

Along the Way

NO FEELINGS

MASTER, I used to feel things keenly
    but now I seem apathetic.
    I can't 'hot-up' over wrongs,
    I can't thrill to joy and beauty.
I seem curiously unresponsive,
    unable to experience emotion,
    as though estranged from life,
watching its current flow by without being immersed in it.

What is wrong, Lord?
Is this a fleeting experience, a temporary depression period?
    Or is it part of the ageing process
    when enthusiasms cool because of lack of energy?
The strings of life have slackened
    so that only flat tones emerge instead of melody
    even when Your fingers play on them.

That's what I'm most concerned about, Master.
I don't feel towards You as I used to do.
    Hymns don't stir me, texts don't move me,
    prayer finds my mind wandering . . .
    I just can't respond.

I am dull, blunted, muted, and suffer from feeling so.
Is this the beginning of petrification,
the turning to stone of what was once a throbbing,
    vibrating heart?

I can't believe it, Lord. I refuse to believe it.
It is something that will pass.
Let me just hold on quietly, believing in You,
loving You with my will if not with my emotions,
    until this mood is over.

Between You and Me, Lord

14 October

AUTUMN ECSTASY

SPRING has its thrill, Master,
> but autumn also has its ecstasy.
It is not only death and decay, it is rebirth.

Even before the leaves fall the embryo buds appear.
Under barren trees lie sodden leaves
thickly piled in a pungent russet carpet
> which shelters new growth,
> feeding the seedlings,
> preparing next year's harvest.
In nature's economy nothing is wasted, nothing lost.

Lord, autumnal shades are very restful to aged eyes.
The sense of fulfilment which broods in nature fills
> my heart too.
There is a rich contentment in which I share,
> a season's cycle completed, a life lived,
> a purpose accomplished.

Look up, my soul, and sing!
For you, too, there are autumn glories.
All is not wasted, all is not finished,
> each end is a beginning!
So will it be for you. Give thanks to God!

Between You and Me, Lord

15 October

INDEPENDENCE

IT'S wrong, Master, I see now that it's wrong,
although all my life I have believed it right.
> I'm too independent!
It can be a kind of pride,
this spirit of 'I can manage on my own'.
It is not the worthy quality it would at first seem.

I ought to have accepted the lady's aid.
> She only wanted to help me
and my cursed independence stood in the way.
Politely, oh so politely, I declined her assistance,
> and went on my way bulging with self-satisfied esteem
Then it struck me, it hit me really hard, Lord,
> that what I had considered a virtue
> was a failing of serious dimension.

186

I was ready to give help but I couldn't accept it,
        not gratefully and graciously.
My pride had erected a barrier of self-sufficiency,
        and that pride was a form of sin.

Help me, Master!
To You I am willing to turn when I stand in need.
Then why can't I accept the kindnesses
        that other people offer me?
Help me to smash this wall of self-sufficing
and to be more responsive to the efforts of others
        to help me along life's path.

Towards You, Lord

16 OCTOBER

GALES

I'M frightened, Lord, of high winds
        when the sky darkens, the windows rattle
and the garden fence sways ominously.
There is something sinister about the unleashed forces of nature.
        At first there is a brooding stillness:
all nature sulking in a sombre hush of dark foreboding.
I note the dull steel colour of the clouds
which herald the approaching storm
        and my heart sinks.

The wind rises and in a few moments the trees
        are bowed before its power,
leaves revealing their pale undersides
like the fluttering of women's petticoats.
The tall masts of the pines sway wisely,
        (better to cede a point than to snap)
while the crash of dead branches accompanies the tinkling
        of tiles falling from the roof.

The heavy rain pelts down and soon a watery sun appears,
        splitting the jagged clouds and girding them with gold.
My mind lifts vigorously to You, Lord.
Help me, Master, when the gales of life buffet me,
        when everything of value seems at risk.
Teach me, like the pines, to bend but not break,
        to be strong yet pliable
        and to live on in hope.

Towards You, Lord

GOOD AND BAD (HARVEST)

LIFE is a series of sowings and reapings.
This is what the years have taught me, Lord.
There are good harvests, bringing joy
        and fulfilment,
but there are also bad ones with their toll
        of heartache and disappointment.

We cast the seeds of acts and words
        so thoughtlessly and lightly,
forgetting that each will germinate, grow
        and bear its own crop.
We are baffled when we reap trouble and discord,
not realising that we ourselves planted the seeds.
Sometimes, though, to our utter surprise
        some happy events reveal their origin
in a few kindly words we spoke
or a friendly deed we did and then forgot.

Harvesting! It is Your law, Master:
        what we sow we inevitably reap,
whether we remember the sowing or not.
Help us then, dear Lord, to be watchful
        over our acts, our words and even our thoughts,
for they too bring a harvest of good or evil.

God in My Everyday

MY PHOBIA – I BLAME THE FOUNDER!

I WAS eight years old when William Booth, Founder of The Salvation Army, died and many Salvationists gathered in the Colston Hall in Bristol for a memorial service.

With my mother and young brother I was seated in one of the top galleries in a tremendously packed hall. I can recall a round building with tiers of boxes and galleries crammed with people, bright lighting everywhere, a fearfully hot atmosphere which I found very unpleasant and a voice droning from the platform against a hushed silence. It was difficult for me to breathe and my heart began to thump. Then I fainted. I came to with someone gripping my wrist hard, while my mother was fanning my face. Then I was carried out.

That incident, unimportant in itself, left an indelible impression on me that a long life has not effaced. In similar circumstances - a round hall, bright

lighting, tiers or galleries of people, silence except for one speaking voice –
and my heart begins to pump hard, I find difficulty in breathing, my hands
grow moist with sweat and I feel deep anxiety. As I grew up I was puzzled
by my reaction to certain meeting halls, but it was years before I pinpointed
the cause through reading that most phobias are caused by some childhood
experience.

Expert opinion is inclined to think that once the cause of a phobia is
found, it should disappear, but that has not been true for me.

Along the Way

FEARS AND PHOBIAS

BE merciful, Lord,
to those who have to live with phobias
or with fears which siphon off courage
yet often cannot be explained.
Some disabilities, physical or mental,
    we must learn to live with,
but oh! the burden to the sufferer.
Some fears can be traced to the trauma
    of an accident, war memories, or a brutal attack.
Suddenly the victim is back again in thought,
    reliving the agonising moments,
    tense and twisted with pain,
    trembling and sweating, left limp and weak.
On each occasion it must be lived through
    then left behind.
It is at least a known trouble.

But, Lord, for those with irrational fears
    there seems no explanation.
Just this agony of depression,
    paralysis of thought, deep despair
and the seeming impossibility of taking action.
Come to such, Lord, with some thought of hope.
If at these moments they cannot pray,
let them hold fast to some promise from Your Word,
some assurance of Your love, Your care.
Even if they cannot feel You near,
let them cling to the hope that one day
    the skies will clear
and the sunshine of Your smile will warm their souls.

My God and I

BECOMING RICH

LORD, today I ponder some wise words:
There are two ways of becoming rich . . .
      to amass possessions
      or to reduce your wants.
The first is closed to me.
Thank You for the common sense which tells me that!
But the second is open . . .
      to reduce my actual needs,
      to see what I can do without
and still live happily.

It can be fun, Lord,
      a kind of permanent challenge
      to a simpler lifestyle,
checking up on what I have
      before acquiring more.
Making over, restyling, making do
      as in wartime economies.

Fortunately I have ceased growing upwards
and I am careful not to grow outward
      by putting on weight.
So my clothes last a long time
      and that is all to the good.
None of this will give me a larger bank balance
but it will give me serenity of mind
      and health of body,
and that is one way of becoming rich.

God in My Everyday

OBSESSED WITH AGE?

FROM Dr Irene Gore's book, *Age and Vitality,* I cite some challenging thoughts: 'Life lived as a continuum is a garnering of enriching experiences. It becomes a process of addition rather than subtraction, of a growing maturity rather than a loss of youth, of evolution rather than dissolution. It removes the pernicious obsession with calendar age which precludes some of us from learning new things, or undertaking new tasks, or taking a new interest in the world around us. The less obsessed with age we are, the more readily we shall go on participating in life.'

Along the Way

POTTED PERTINENCE

ANOTHER bit of wisdom, which surely most of us recognise:

> *Half of my life was rendered sad*
> *By thinking, 'How I wish I had!'*
> *The other half was fairly maddened*
> *By thinking, 'How I wish I hadn't!'*

Along the Way

TIRED OF BEING UNSELFISH

I'M tired of being unselfish, Master;
tired of taking the burnt toast,
      the cracked cup,
      the squashed tomato,
      the broken fish,
      the bruised banana,
      the smallest egg and so on.

It doesn't make me any less selfish either,
for I get a kick out of 'denying myself',
hearing silent applause of me by me
      in the back of my mind.

So I'm tired of being unselfish, Lord,
tired of being compulsively unselfish, that is;
      urging myself from within,
      always working against the grain,
      and ever forcing the issue.

I want something better, something higher, something nobler,
something that only You can give me.
      I want a love for others
      that will make me want to give them the best;
      that their good shall be my delight
      and their joy my reward.

Is it too much to ask of You, Master,
this outgoing love that will make me forget myself,
so that I no longer think of 'denying myself'
(Self is happy to parade even under that banner)?
A positive love, not a negative restraint . . .
Lord, in Your rich mercy will You grant me this?

Just a Moment, Lord

SLANDER

MALICIOUS slander may wound deeply
       and scar a woman's soul.
You, Lord, who welcomed the ministry of women
       among Your followers
set a high value upon their devotion to You
       and Your cause.
You knew too how vulnerable a woman can be
because of her sensitivity and intuition.

Evil tongues wagged about You, Master,
calling You a glutton and a drunkard,
so You understand what suffering
       venomous backbiting can bring.
If the woman is a Christian she will try to forgive,
but oh! how difficult that can be!
       To hold one's head high,
to go resolutely about the daily tasks
knowing of the whispering behind one's back;
hearing the innuendoes in conversation,
being shunned by former friends
       all because of evil lies.

You triumphed, Lord! Not only over slander
but right through to the tragedy of the cross,
and there You could whisper:
       'Father, forgive them!'
Such love we would fain share, Master,
but it is impossible in our own strength.
Only the spirit of Your love in our hearts
       can bring us to forgive.
May our souls be bathed in Your love,
so that at last we can pray for those
       who have wronged us.

My God and I

ODD ONE OUT

SOME people, Lord, are not good mixers.
They are awkward in company and prefer
       to be alone.
It is not simple shyness but a feeling
of being otherwise, the odd one out.

This sense of isolation can bring
　　　　real suffering, intense though hidden.
One may feel an outsider in the home
or in an office where everyone is known.

Does being different from others
　　　　bring alienation, Master?
Is such a person on another wavelength
and so cannot absorb what others contribute
　　　　in good-natured chat?
Is feeling the odd one out a permanent
　　　　or passing stage?

Are there ways to bridge the gulf with fellow-men?
One thing is certain, Lord.
There are no outsiders in Your Kingdom!
　　　　All are welcome, all share Your love.
Should not the odd one out make an effort
to find some small group with which to mingle
and perhaps in time to feel at ease?
Help me to be on the lookout
　　　　for any loners,
and, with a smile or friendly nod, to lessen their isolation.

My God and I

26 OCTOBER

A GOOD TURN A DAY

MUCH interest and even adventure can be added to life if we will adopt the simple procedure of doing someone a good turn each day. This may sound like a Scout programme, but that should not make it unacceptable.

Some time ago a widow with few friends and no relatives was working hard at home to support herself and her small son. Letters were rare in her life and she was surprised one day to receive a letter from New Zealand. She knew no one there. Yet her name and her address were correctly written on the envelope. Inside was a lovely lace-edged handkerchief with a red rose and the words 'with love'.

Weeks later she told an acquaintance of this experience. 'Why,' said her friend, 'that must be from so-and-so out there to whom I send our local paper. It carries names and addresses of those who are bereaved. She must have felt led to send you an anonymous gift to cheer you up.'

The mystery was solved, but an act of kindness had brightened a woman's life, and would be long remembered.

Hints for Living

EAST WIND

I'M a barometer, Master, up and down with the weather,
    changeful as the sunshine flecked with passing clouds.
I can predict storms, rain, frost and snow by feeling them in my bones
    and an east wind gives me the grouse.

I'm then no longer on top of things;
    the world is a hostile place and people filled with evil intentions.
I thought Mrs Grey was so kind yesterday
    but today I see through her devices.
I was pleased with the joint I bought
    but now it appears all gristle and bone

The biggest change, though, is in my relationship to You.
Yesterday I was sure of Your love;
    today I see no evidence of it.
Yesterday I felt You understood me, accepted me;
    today I feel an outcast from Your care.

Can a wind, an east wind, do this to me?
Am I so frail, so vulnerable, that a harsh wind
    can drive me to the point of desperation?

Stop complaining, I say to myself, don't spread your gloomy views,
    others are feeling the weather just as much as you are.
Refuse to give in to the angry blustering wind,
    it can't change facts but only feelings.
Hold on to your facts and your feelings will sort themselves out
as soon as the sun struggles through.

Lord, I don't want this to happen again.
I don't want to be an old curmudgeon, grousing the days through.
Help me, please, to conquer my low feelings,
    knowing that they are only a passing phase.

Between You and Me, Lord

WRINKLES

WE have to accept the features we are born with, but the expression on our face becomes our own as the years go by. It is said that by the time we are 60 we have the looks we deserve!

    We begin life with a spring face, which in middle life becomes a summer face, and then for our later years we bear our autumn face.

Cosmetics might possibly slow up the appearance of wrinkles in some slight measure, but finally they will appear. Why should we be ashamed of them? They are nature's seal upon our maturity. They are signs that we have *lived*!

Hints for Living

BONDAGE

LORD, I am not free!
I live in perpetual bondage to tradition,
      to tight schedules,
      to imposed priorities.
I am hemmed in by precedent and convention,
      hampered by prejudice . . . and I rebel!

Some of these are necessary.
      That I accept, Master.
I am one in a team and I must play my part
      and accept my responsibilities.
But is my loyalty to the group greater than
      my devotion to You, Lord?
Is my concern for the success of our venture
      swayed by personal ambition,
      or zeal for Your Kingdom?

At times I feel a slave to duty,
working mechanically in well-defined ways
having bludgeoned my mind to only one thought –
      to keep going at full stretch.
I have made a fetish of duty –
      a swollen, unrealistic idol
      which I can never satisfy.
Where is the freedom You promised, Lord?

All right! I accept Your rebuke –
      I will slow down . . .
A breath of Your deep calm quiets my heart;
instead of me working my fingers to the bone
      for You,
You will direct my energies into a controlled pattern,
allowing time for recreation, reading and fellowship.
Thus I shall become a better worker,
with less risk of a breakdown.

God in My Everyday

IT COSTS TO CARE

IT costs to care, Master!
You know that well Yourself.
Your love made You vulnerable to misunderstandings
        among Your followers,
brought You contempt, opposition and hatred
        from religious leaders,
and led You to a cross and a painful death.

Even I know that it costs to care, Lord.
Every tie of love with another creates a tender area
        where a blow might fall.
To enlarge the circle of one's family,
        to increase the number of one's friends,
is to offer oneself to possible bruising of spirit.

It hurts to love!
It is easier to close in upon oneself and shut others out;
        and yet I pray, O Lord,
expand my heart to embrace more people,
        although it might cause pain;
widen the narrow channels of my love, so choked
        with debris of my own concerns.
Let Your surging power sweep through, cleansing,
        deepening and broadening my affections,
until I am more capable of loving,
        and therefore more capable of suffering,
until I know the high cost of caring.

It is the way of the cross, Master,
        the way You went.
Help me to follow in Your steps

Towards You, Lord

PICK A POSY FOR YOUR SOUL

WHY not wear an invisible buttonhole, a choice flower or thought that we pick for our soul each morning? It can be a word or phrase from the Bible or from a favourite song or poem. With this nosegay safely tucked away within us we will have something to think about when we are kept waiting, something on which to stay our soul throughout the day.

Along the Way

ALL SOULS' DAY

TODAY is All Souls' Day and in Scandinavia the cemeteries are scenes of great activity as families visit the graves and lay evergreen wreaths and light candles. In the gloom of winter the sight of these hundreds of candles flickering in the wind stirs strong emotions.

Language changes and words acquire new meaning. Last century a town or village was reported to have so many 'souls'. A ship was said to have capsized with all souls on board, and SOS signals for help reiterated 'save our *souls*'. And we can still write that 'not a soul was astir on that quiet evening'. All the time we mean people.

This thought gives new meaning to William Booth's oft quoted challenge: 'Go for souls and go for the worst.' He meant go for people. Love for souls, sounding so spiritual, so ethereal, so nebulous, simply means love for people – anybody and everybody.

Surely not that awful Mrs Green in the next street? Oh no, Lord! I can love her soul but not the woman herself, for strangely enough it is possible to 'love souls' at a safe distance, while avoiding nearby people. So instead of talking of winning souls, can't we speak clearly of winning people for Christ and thus bring greater clarity into our evangelistic efforts?

Along the Way

THROUGH THE CLOUDS

ON returning by air from Copenhagen, my plane had to dive into a bank of cloud as we neared Heathrow. From the brilliant sunshine we dipped into swirling grey mist and words from Robert Browning's *Paracelsus* came to my mind:

> *If I stoop*
> *Into a dark tremendous sea of cloud,*
> *It is but for a time; I press God's lamp*
> *Close to my breast; its splendour, soon or late,*
> *Will pierce the gloom; I shall emerge one day.*

God's lamp is the spark of faith He quickens in our hearts. In any period of gloom or doubt it is good to remind ourselves, 'I shall emerge one day.'

Along the Way

PLAN FOR A DULL DAY

FROM an anonymous source I have picked up a good three-point plan for a dull day: GET UP, CHEER UP AND CLEAR UP. Not a bad idea!

Along the Way

THINGS POSSESS ME

LORD, I've made a disappointing discovery.
Things possess me:
I'd always tried to believe that I was the ascetic type;
  not the real ascetic, of course,
  facts were against that,
  but with tendencies in that direction.
Now I find that what is mine is very important to me,
  even if it is not of any great worth.

It must be Great-aunt Maria behind this, Lord,
for she was a miser if ever there was one.
  Bits of old string, paper bags,
  empty boxes and bottles . . .
Those were some of her more harmless acquisitions,
and I find that I can't throw them away without wincing.

I don't want to be bound by things, Lord;
  to use, yes;
  to enjoy, yes;
  to lend, sometimes;
  but to hoard, simply to gloat over their possession, no!
Your Book tells us a few home truths, Master.
It reminds us that even as we brought nothing into this world,
So we depart, empty-handed.
It makes one think.

There must be some secret formula to follow,
  to hold in trust, to use wisely,
  to treasure unpossessively and be ready to surrender.
I have a lot to learn, Lord;
  please teach me how to sit lightly to this world's goods.

Just a Moment, Lord

JEALOUSY

A PRIEST once said, 'The only sin I've never heard anyone confess to is jealousy.' The poison, jealousy, affects the mind, heart and also the body, bringing illness in its train. Some think that jealousy is caused by love; that one is jealous because one loves deeply.

That is not true.

Jealousy is caused by self-love, a very different thing. If we love anyone we think of their best, we trust them, we want them to enjoy themselves. If self-love fills our heart we are saying to ourselves: 'Why should he go there when I have to stay at home?' 'Why should she visit her friends when I am not invited?'

Jealousy is not caused by what happens outside you.

It is a fault, a sin, within you. It is how you think about things. To conquer it you must be willing to admit that you are jealous and to name to yourself the person you are jealous of. Then ask God to forgive you for having given that jealous feeling place in your thoughts.

Hints for Living

YOUR LOVE IS STERN

YOUR love is stern, Lord,
steel-centred and unyielding.
It envelops me gently but it challenges me straitly.
There is no soft sentimentality about it;
  no fond blindness to faults,
  no condoning of disobedience,
  no deafness to disloyalty
  or minimising of wrongdoing.

You are not like an indulgent father who says:
  'Never mind what the children do,
  as long as they enjoy themselves.'

Your purpose is not my enjoyment
  but my development;
  my development in Christian character.

You set tests and tasks to be performed.
  You discipline, and demand results.
  You pull, push and prick until I fain would cry out:
   'Enough! Leave me.'

But You won't leave me, will You, Master?
  Even when I am most rebellious,
  when I writhe and squirm,
  when I protest most loudly,
for it is then that I most need You, Lord.

Your love is stern, Master,
  but I would not have it otherwise.
  You have set Yourself a hard task,
  trying to make a sinner into a saint.

Just a Moment, Lord

ON THE SIDELINES

I'VE been transferred to the sidelines, Master!
No more for me the taxing schedule,
   the demanding duties,
   the heavy pressures.
I have been thanked for past service
(and how well my record was made to sound!).
Then I was duly retired, so now
   I stand on the sidelines,
watching the surgings of the game of life.

It was a great relief, Lord, at first . . .
   to relax,
   call time my own;
   to plan or not to plan,
   to go out or stay in just as I wished.

Then came a feeling of emptiness,
   of something lacking.
To think that one could become weary of resting!

How shall I fill up time, Master?
Shall I fill it like a Christmas stocking
with lots of goodies and small delights?
Or shall I heroically choose a demanding course,
   a complicated hobby
   or some social involvement?
You must help me to decide aright, Lord,
for the years of my life which lie ahead
   might be many,
and I would not have them
   worthlessly frittered away.

God in My Everyday

SITTING LIGHTLY TO LIFE

HELP me, Lord, to sit lightly to life,
to be ready to rise from my place
   when the summons comes to meet You,
   empty-handed and alone.

Let my grasp loosen on my few possessions.
Don't let me try to lug them with me, Lord,

clambering up the Heavenly staircase
clutching my dainty fruit knives
and some favourite books
and trailing my tape recorder.
Other spheres will have other treasures
so let me go in glad anticipation of what awaits me.

Let me leave my garden to another's care,
glad for the days when I could tend it,
grateful for colour and fragrance,
not grudging the hours of toil it entailed
but considering them an investment for someone else's pleasure.

My home I thank You for, Master. I have needed its shelter.
During years it has been a comfortable shell
round my vulnerable body
but now I must leave it.
Let me throw a glance of recognition around,
grateful for all memories.

Let me wave a plucky farewell to my dear ones,
those who are left
for most have gone before,
knowing that I shall meet them again in Your presence.

So I sit lightly to life, Master,
awaiting Your summons whenever You send for me.

Between You and Me, Lord

DOING WITHOUT

A FEW anonymous lines pinpoint a very valuable lesson for us all in the art of doing without:

You can't do as you like? Then do as you can;
I'm sure you will find it the very best plan.
Can't have what you want? Take what you can get,
No better device has been patented yet.
'Tis the bravest and blithest and best way by far
Not to let little losses your happiness mar.
'Tis an art that needs practice,
of that there's no doubt,
But 'tis worth it –
this fine art of doing without.

Along the Way

RAPTURE

I'M waiting, Lord,
waiting quietly and expectantly before You.
You have said:
    'Be still and know that I am God.'
So I calm my restive thoughts – as far as I can –
    and sit relaxed.
I think of You, Lord of life,
    Saviour and King,
I praise You and thank You,
    then again I wait . . .

In swift action You respond,
    startling me for an instant;
a surge of rapture thrills through my being,
I feel myself invaded by Your Spirit,
    filled with joy and love.
A sea of blessedness laps round me,
    engulfs me,
    bears me on its waves,
a sense of mental and spiritual well-being vibrates through me,
    out to my very fingertips.
I worship and adore!

Moments or minutes? I don't know!
I only know that You have made contact with me,
that for a brief interval I have been more spirit than body.
Now I not only believe, I know.
    In exultation I rejoice in You.
As I return to waiting tasks
    a serene joy remains with me.
I walk as on air
    for You have revealed Yourself to me.

Between You and Me, Lord

PREVIEW OF SPRING

IT was lovely one dull November morning to get an unexpected preview of
spring. It made my day. I had taken the garden fork to dig up some of the
luxuriant grass invading the rose plot, having found the hoe inadequate for
the deep roots. Suddenly my fork turned up a heavy lump of something with
long shoots pressing upward. I found it was a clump of daffodil bulbs, and

the tips of the long shoots were already greening as they neared the surface. Very hurriedly I planted them again, remembering that I had placed them there to bloom while the roses enjoyed their winter rest. I hope the bulbs were not seriously disturbed but I was jubilant to see them so far advanced.

I felt I had enjoyed a preview of springtime.

Along the Way

PACKING AND UNPACKING

I DISLIKE packing, Master,
though I regard myself as something of an expert
    after a lifetime of travelling.
The biggest difficulty is deciding what to take,
without knowing all the possible factors:
    the likely weather – very important!
    the possible duties – best to be prepared;
    alternative routes – in case of strikes,
    extra money – sure to be needed.

But even worse than packing for a journey
    is the unpacking after homecoming.
Everything crumpled, creased and semi-soiled.
Why can't we have throwaway luggage
    like we have disposable picnic sets?
Just imagine buying a weekend set of holiday clothes
    complete in your own size,
then casting it into the dustbin before travelling home,
    empty-handed but light-hearted.

My thoughts go to the final packing,
    for the journey from which there is no return.
Or is it rather an unpacking, Master?
The dumping of unfulfilled hopes, of half-made plans,
    of tiresome frustrations and petty vexations,
    slamming the lid on a box of grudges.
Away with them all, I've finished with them . . .
    then turning my face to the light,
lifting my heart to You in final yielding,
and empty-handed, passing through the veil
into the eternal spheres where You await,
    My Saviour, Lord and King.

Towards You, Lord

THE HYDRA-HEADED MONSTER

YOU said some strange things, Master,
    things that I often ponder.
You said that a man must deny himself
    if he would follow You.

But self has more lives than any cat!
That is what experience has taught me, Lord.
It is a hydra-headed monster,
making a resolute comeback from every knock-out blow.

Talk of split personality!
      We're all split into fractions,
      pulled in several directions at once.

Your task is to integrate us, Lord,
    to make of many bits a whole,
    and a decent whole;
cementing the various parts by one dominant purpose;
    to live according to Your laws and plans
    with self as obedient servant.

Self as servant and not as master?
    Try it out and see.
Just put the old fellow off his throne
and You'll have a lot of trouble on Your hands.

Master, this is going to be a daily battle,
a stand-up fight to the death.
Help me not to weary of it,
not to tire of slaying the foe within,
for I want to follow You.

Just a Moment, Lord

HIDDEN TREASURE

I HAVE a lovely secret, Master,
    one that I hug closely to my heart
shared only with You and two others, both of them gardeners.
I came upon them one dull November morning in the park.
    They were working swiftly, burying a treasure.
With small trowels they made holes each side of the path
and deep in the holes they hid hyacinth bulbs.

Ten minutes later when I passed the spot again
the bare brown earth stared unwinkingly at me
          as though to say: 'There's nothing here.'
But I had seen and I knew.

I hugged my delicious secret to my breast all winter long,
allowing myself only swift glances to right and left
          as I passed the spot.
I felt like the man in Your Book, Master,
who stumbled upon treasure in a field
          and who hastily covered it over;
then with his face all innocence
he bargained and bought the field,
          knowing what lay under the rough surface.

I, too, know and wait . . .
My heart glows with glad anticipation every time I pass.
One day my treasure will appear
          and many others will share it with me
as part of Your wonderful spring bounty, Lord.
O Creator God, I worship You.
Lord of life in its myriad forms and fashions,
granting us joys and satisfactions untold
in the rhythm of the yearly growth cycle,
          my heart rejoices in Your power.

Between You and Me, Lord

A NEW PARKINSON'S LAW

I HAVE discovered a new Parkinson's law, one I am sure the great man would have discovered for himself, had he been a housewife. My new contribution to the world's astounding facts is this:

Contents of cupboards expand to overflow the space allotted to them.

I have proved this theory again and again. Cupboards and drawers are never big enough to take what should go in them. They take it to start with, but by some strange alchemy the contents expand and multiply, until one is forced to action. The cupboard or drawer is cleared out, sorted and refilled neatly and tidily, each thing in its place. But by its side lies a pile of cast-offs, which need another home. It is only by great strength of will that I can sometimes consign them to a jumble sale or to the dustbin.

Along the Way

GLISTENING PEARLS

FOG is a pest, Lord!
It dampens, distorts and dribbles.
It blankets the soul as well as the body.
I had to go out shopping, and so must face it.
As I put on a warm coat and gloves I little guessed
        what was awaiting me outside.

On the yew tree near my front door hung
        dozens of fairy festoons of spiders' webs;
each frail thread outlined with minute drops of water
        glistening like pearls.
I was riveted, enthralled by the sight
and stood in utter enjoyment
of the unexpected beauty.

But duty called and I left on my errands.
When I returned the sun had broken through
        and gone were the pearls!
The webs must still have been there but they were now invisible.
I had the memory, though, of the magic sight
and I said a hearty thank You, Lord,
        giver of all good gifts,
        author of all beauty.

                        My God and I

MY VISITING LIST

MY visiting list is restricted, Master.
        It might be called selective.
There are family calls, friendly calls and duty visits
        when people are ill or in trouble.
But *You* are also on my list, Lord.
I call at Your house each Sunday morning,
        hoping to find You in.
I dress especially for the occasion in my best clothes
        and I always go prepared to listen
        to what You have to say,
although I rarely receive any direct message.

In addition I am 'at home' to You each morning after breakfast
        for a set time,
when I read Your Book, meditate and pray.

If I fail in this I feel I must apologise to You.
So what is missing, Master? Isn't this enough?
What more can You expect?
Why should my heart feel cold when I have
such a good working programme with You?
Ah! I know the answer, Lord.
These splendid commitments are but the externals,
the cool technique, the duty run.
What You desire is the loving look,
the quick lifting of the heart at any moment of the day –
to thank, to praise or to worship mutely.
I have kept the outward form without the strong intent.
Pardon me, Lord!
Let me not give You less time but rather put more ardour
into my search for You
and Your companionship in my every day.

God in My Everyday

DIVORCE

MARITAL breakdowns leave many scars:
deep caverns of self-doubt,
flashes of bitter resentment, pockets of self-blame
and the painful wound of rejection.
O God, be very near to those who know
the anguish of divorce,
the searing pain of loneliness
complicated by the care of children and financial worries.

It is the end of something which began so well.
Love, joy, companionship . . . What went wrong?
Too late now to question and analyse.
The break has been made final.
All that is left is to pick up the pieces and start life afresh.

O God of hope, of new beginnings,
grant to all divorced persons the immense courage
needed to face the future.
May they do so relying on Your strength and guidance.
In spite of inward stress and torment may they commit themselves
to Your care, trusting You to help them work out
a future better than the past.

My God and I

MY SHADOW

I'M uneasy about my shadow, Lord.
     Not the shadow cast by light,
but the invisible shadow which is my influence.
Wherever I go this silent presence creeps after me,
mingles with my friends when we converse,
yet still flits around when I am silent.
It is short, touching those closest to me,
yet long, oh so long,
                        stretching right into the distance,
affecting known and unknown people . . .
and I can't control its action.

That is a serious thought, Lord.
I can never say: 'Today I will exert a good influence.'
        My shadow would mock me.
        It has a life of its own,
linked and dependent on mine, it is true,
yet far freer, mobile and self-determining.

The aura of what I am pervades
        what I do and say.
It sometimes nullifies my best endeavours,
        sets at nought my well-laid plans,
        puts obstacles in my way
and shouts aloud when I command silence.

What can I do, Master,
about this shadow which is my influence on others?
Will You so dwell within me in the fullness
     of Your Spirit,
that my life is under Your control?
Then I need not fear the effect
of my invisible shadow falling on others.

Towards You, Lord

ANOTHER NEW PARKINSON'S LAW

I WOULD like to offer another such law, the result of my own experience. It is that *events attract events*. You must have noticed how, after several weeks or months of quiet living, you are suddenly visited by a succession of friends and relatives in the course of a few days. If you have planned a holiday, that is just the time that you receive a notice to attend hospital for some long-delayed treatment.

Or a friend from overseas visits Britain, just when you have gone abroad for a change. Months of uneventfulness are followed by hectic days of trying to sort all kinds of happenings into a pattern of possible achievement. And you long for quiet, peaceful days again. They are surely on their way.

Along the Way

QUICK RESULTS

WE live in quick-result days, Master.
Desirable goods can be obtained
      by pressing a button,
      opening a tin
      or defrosting a packet.
As long as one can pay, one can obtain
      instant satisfaction.

Suntan without sun is promised
by the simple application of a cream or spray.
You lie down marked with winter's pallor
to arise as from a holiday on a sunny beach,
      glowingly, faultlessly, tanned all over.

We are spoiled, Lord, by this ability to take quick cuts,
      to pay in money
      rather than in effort;
to achieve easy counterfeits which look
      like the real thing.
But that is not possible with spiritual values.
There are no short cuts to holiness of life,
no funiculars up the mountain of Christian character.
It is easy to *look* good, simple to *sound* good,
quite possible to *feel* good, without *being* good.

O God, help me to be the real thing!
Clear out the subterfuges in my life.
      Let me be sincere and open,
not pretending to be more than I am
      or other than I am,
yet steadily progressing along the Christian pathway.

Towards You, Lord

UNFINISHED THINGS

TODAY, Lord, I see my life like a highway.
I look back and, as far as memory can trace,
I see unfinished things thrown aside.
I have been a veritable litterbug in this respect.

>The thrill of starting something fresh;
>the enthusiasm for a new idea;
>the joy of creating;
>then the slackening of interest as the new venture
>>palled.
>
>Laying it aside; forgetting it for many days:
>and finally throwing it away.

It's not wrong, Lord, to have thrown so much aside.
The fault was in beginning too much.

>As a child it is good to try one's skills;
>but adults must discriminate.

If I accept this, I must relinquish that;
if I give time to this, I must sacrifice that;
if I choose this, I must renounce that.

>I need wisdom, Master.
>I need Your help, Your guidance.

For I have only one life to live,
only so much time invested in the bank of life,
and I want my life to count.

>To count for good;
>to accomplish something useful;
>to help bring in Your Kingdom.

Show me, then, what things are worthwhile, Lord,
and help me do them with all my heart and mind.

Just a Moment, Lord

GOD-MOMENTS

LORD, teach me to make brief pauses
>in the rhythm of my days,
to quiet my mind, relax my muscles
>and rest my soul.

Life is so wearing!
	So continual and persistent.
The minutes trudge on mechanical feet
	throughout the hours,
pacing out the passage of time
	with unrelenting doom.
At times I gasp for a space,
	a pause in the steady pressure,
but then I realise, Master, that only I
	can create brief breaks
in the monotony of routine.

So I ask for Your help, Lord.
Teach me to make pauses,
	brief but effective breaks
	for God-moments.
A winged prayer for Your blessing,
	murmured thanks for Your love,
	a swift uplook into Your face,
a nestling into Your tender care.

There will be no chance for more
While duties demand their toll of time,
	but this small sacred oasis
	will refresh my heart
and keep me close to You.
Master, teach me the value of God-moments
	throughout my day.

God in My Everyday

24 NOVEMBER

LOVELY!

RECENTLY I have been astonished by the frequent and surprising use of the word 'lovely!' In as small a matter as telephoning for a shampoo and set, the assistant gave me a time, then added, 'Lovely! Goodbye!'

The next day, in a rather protracted and painful experience (for me) at the dentist, he kept uttering 'lovely!' in a cheerful voice, probably calculated to calm my fears. He even hummed a few bars of 'Onward, Christian soldiers' under his breath, finishing up with another resounding 'lovely!'

I survived . . .

Along the Way

PETITIONS

I SEE You, Master, holding the lines of many prayers in
              Your hands,
simple prayers, brief prayers, wordless prayers,
as well as verbose petitions from which You
              must sift the real purport,
and weaving these prayers together as a strong strand
              to which the needy can cling.

What a privilege You have given us, Lord, to be able
              to pray for our dear ones,
knowing that Your tender care stretches out to embrace
              them wherever they may be
and that You will somehow use our prayers for succour
              in an hour of stress.

Do You have a prayer bank, Lord?
What do You do with those vague requests that accomplish little
              because they ask nothing definite?
Do You store them up in a Heavenly repository
              until the quantity makes up for lack of quality?
It is an interesting question,
              but I must leave the answer to You.

Today I send my prayer winging up to You
              for my loved ones far away.
I name each one before You
              knowing that You care for them personally.
By faith I place them in the golden light of Your love,
that constant stream of divine mercy which embraces all,
              and my heart is comforted
              because I leave them in Your hands.

Thank You, Master, for that favour.

Between You and Me, Lord

ARE YOU COMFORTABLE?

LIKE 'lovely' another overworked, misleading word is 'comfortable'.

    This broadminded expression lends itself to multifarious use, such as,
'After the amputation of both legs, the patient was reported to be
"comfortable".' Or again, 'Badly bruised and with several broken ribs, the
woman was admitted to hospital where she is now said to be "comfortable".'

And how are you today? You may have migraine, arthritis, influenza or perhaps an ingrown toenail, but surely you are 'comfortable'?

That must be a comforting thought!

Along the Way

PEARLS AND PIGS

WHAT did You mean, Master, when You said:
    'Don't feed pearls to pigs'?
It's quite obvious that it can't be taken literally.
    It was figurative talking
as so much else that came from Your lips,
    difficult to grasp with a Westerner's dull intuition.

It's clear that 'pearls' are things of great value,
    and 'pigs' . . . ?
    they must be people.
    Not very complimentary!

In essence, Lord, it seems that You say we should not
        offer to people
    what they can't appreciate.
If they want mush and swill and straw,
    well, give them that, anything else would be wasted.

Then, Lord, how is it that You gave Yourself,
    Your love, Your life, for humankind?
Wasn't that offering pearls to pigs,
    something of infinite worth
    to those unable to value it?

But You did it, Lord,
    and for that we thank You,
we thank You with brimming eyes and grateful hearts.
You saw beneath our outward, brutish being,
    You saw the spark of the divine
    within the grasping, selfish pig-heart.
You cast Your pearls with reckless abandon,
    risking Your all for the sake of love.

Some of us want to thank You, Lord,
for offering so much to us of little worth.
From the depths of my heart I thank You personally.

Between You and Me, Lord

213

THE 'FLU

I'VE got it, Master, and it's got me,
    got me tight.
Aching and shivering I lie in bed
as far down in spirits as I've ever been.
I rack my brain: when did I catch it?
    why did I catch it?
    There is no answer
for I am too tired to work it out.

How can a sane, healthy person be reduced to this
    state in a few hours?
I'm invaded by a virus waving a victor's flag.
Where are my own body defences?
Why didn't they get busy to repel the enemy?
    Were they caught napping?
    Or overwhelmed?

Here I lie, a veritable battlefield
    and feeling like one.
It's not only a physical ordeal but a spiritual one.
    You seem far away, Lord.
    I can't pray,
    I can't respond to You.
    I can't even think!

I sigh disconsolately, then I remember something.
I'm not holding on to You, Master,
    it's You who is holding on to me!
So even if I feel nothing it doesn't change our
    relationship.
My emotions are sick but Your loving care still
    encircles me
and I rest in the shelter of Your arms
even when I can't feel them around me.

You won't mind me not praying to You today, Master?
I can't control my thoughts and feelings;
so help me just to rest in Your love
    until this sickness is over.

Between You and Me, Lord

THIS FELLOW

YOU had many taunts flung at You, Master,
          as You trod this earth of ours.
Insults, scorn and hatred flourished round You,
          but perhaps the most barbed of all
          were the contemptuous words:
'This fellow welcomes bad people and eats with them.'

It was intended as a smack in the face for You, Lord.
          You went to parties and weddings,
          as well as to sick-beds and funerals.
          At one time You were quite popular
          and even sought after,
but You were not very discriminating
          in the type of folk You mixed with,
          so they thought You didn't know.

Didn't know that rich clothing hid a grasping, selfish heart,
          that flowing robes concealed a harlot's body;
that compliments were but the grappling irons of a trap,
          a trap to catch You,
          and kill You.

As though You didn't know . . .
You with the steady eyes that saw through people,
with the keen perception that weighed motives and quickly summed
up character.

You gave them an answer:
what was meant as a gibe, You took as a compliment.
          You put Your cards on the table
          and told them straight out:
'I'm not looking for good people, but for bad.'
They hated You all the more for that remark,
          for it baffled them.

But it gives us courage to come to You, Master.
We know that You welcome such as we are.
You welcome crooked characters to put them straight,
You welcome the sick at heart to make them well,
You welcome sinners to make them saints.
You welcome me. For that I thank You.

Just a Moment, Lord

215

30 NOVEMBER

LIVE WITH FAITH

WE have so often been told that we must have faith, that many of us accept it as a general proposition. Most of us, however, say wistfully: 'I wish I had more faith.'

I often have the feeling that when people pray to God to increase their faith, they expect to receive come kind of a package from Heaven, something like a tin of 'Instant Faith' that they can strew on their daily lives to pep them up a little. It would be very convenient if that were possible. I think, though, that God has another way of increasing our faith.

He will increase it when we use the faith we have. In other words, it is something that we *practise* until it gets stronger and more reliable within us.

Faith in itself is nothing except a link. The power comes from what I place my faith in. People have placed their faith – and their money – in banks and been left bankrupt. Others have placed their faith in a home remedy for coughs that grandmother used to use, and found that it did not work.

It was not the faith that was at fault but the object of the faith. Here we come to the right solution to our problems of faith. If we place our faith in God and his faithfulness, then we shall never be deceived, for he is true and reliable.

'Have faith in God,' the Bible tells us. This faith is not simply a general belief in a creed. That is good to have. But faith to live on must be active, must concern the small details of our everyday lives as well as the great spiritual truths. I must believe that God cares about me now, that he listens to my prayers today, that he is interested in my affairs at this very moment. In that way faith becomes a living link between God and me and through it he is able to send that guidance, that comfort, that strength I need.

If you want to learn to live with faith you must turn to the Bible. Read some of the great texts that speak of trust in God and relying on his help, and then live out those texts in the circumstances of your daily life. Feed these great messages of faith into your mind. Say them over and over again to yourself. Write them on slips of paper and keep them in your purse or wallet. Then there is hope that your faith will grow for you will be learning to use it. And living with faith will make all the difference to your life.

Hints for Living

DANGLING LEAVES

I SAW them in the park this morning, Lord,
    and I chuckled to myself, for I'm just like them.
Other leaves had withered and fallen,
    obeying nature's mysterious laws,
but a few individualists remained dangling on the branches,
weathered pennants of a season's storms.
    Withered, yes, their rich colours fading,
    but still alive
    and – if leaves can kick – kicking.

They were enjoying themselves dancing in the autumnal gusts
    and my heart danced with them.
They exulted in the strong wind, even mocked it, I felt,
    for still they hung on,
    grimly but triumphantly.
My season is over too, Lord, but *I* hang on
with sufficient strength and humour to make it worth while.
    The sap of life still flows in my veins,
    enough to withstand life's tempests.
Though wrinkled and faded, I'm still game.

One day some harsh frost or boisterous wind
    will get the better of me.
My tenuous hold on life will snap
    and my body will return to the soil where it belongs,
    yielding itself willingly to Mother Earth
    while my spirit returns to You.
Until then, Master, keep my courage high.
Let me play the game right to the finish
    then not quarrel when the end comes.
It's been a good life, Master, with Your aid.

Between You and Me, Lord

PROBLEMS

MOST of us have problems, even children, it seems. My four-year-old grandson once confided earnestly to me over the meal table. 'I don't like my dinner, but I do like ice-cream. That's my problem.'

    I'm afraid the future will hold many more serious problems than that – but children's problems are real, just the same.

Along the Way

TIME

WHAT has happened to time, Master?
The clock ticks on as usual
    but the measure of its hours seems erratic.
When I was young there was a vast expanse of time
    between sunrise and sunset,
    enough to live a whole life in,
    each moment crammed with activity.
Now a day slips by unobtrusively
    without leaving any trace of its passing.
    It is here, then gone.

As a child I thought eternity stretched
    from one Christmas to the next,
the monotony of slowly passing months
    only broken by a brief summer holiday.
Now I hardly put the seasonal decorations away
    before it is time to unbox them again.

Time appears to be elastic, Lord,
stretching or contracting in a disconcerting way.
The waiting for a telephone call or a letter
    is time spun out to its thinnest thread
    and longest dimension
but hours of joyous fellowship flit hastily by,
    compacted into utter brevity.

This teaches me one thing, Master . . .
not to reckon life by passing days but by true living.
One single hour can contain more of value than a year.
Help me, Lord, to remain vital and responsive,
    interested and involved,
receiving the precious hours as a gift from You
    to be enjoyed as they slip away.

Between You and Me, Lord

DEMOLITION

LORD, it's rather painful to watch demolition,
old walls giving way under the bulldozer's assaults,
    violent house-death with paroxysms of collapsing walls
    in choking clouds of dust.

Bedroom walls still festooned with flowery paper
      gape open like outrageous wounds.
People have lived there, loved there,
      borne their children and laid out their dead.
There is romance, tragedy, laughter and tears
      woven into the fabric of the building
      now torn apart and destroyed.

In former days buildings mellowed and decayed,
leaky roof, rotting floors, gaping window frames,
      were not attractive to see
but birds, mice and beetles found homes there,
      the ruins gradually melting into the landscape
      towards final decay.

Harsh modern demolition makes place for new homes
      in ever-growing communities.
Let it be done swiftly, then,
      swiftly and noisily if need be, soon over.

Something new will come.
Neat modern houses with frilly curtains at polished panes,
young couples, pensioners, families with teenagers.
Looking into the future I pray for them.
      May they be happy here!
May their homes represent shelter and security
      as well as comfort and love.
Lord, let Your blessing rest upon the new households,
      right from the day they move in.

Between You and Me, Lord

5 DECEMBER
THE DRUMBEAT OF THE SPIRIT

THOREAU wrote: 'If a man does not keep pace with his companion, perhaps it is because he hears another drummer.' We who are Christians hear the drumbeat of the Spirit of God and therefore of necessity we walk at a different pace from those who follow their own plans.

To be in step with God often means to be out of step with the world. At times it might mean being out of step with other Christians who do not interpret the Bible as we do, but at least they are going in the same direction. We shall not hear God's drumbeat if we are walking with radio music blaring in our ears. There are times when we must listen to God, to hear what he is saying to us.

Along the Way

6 DECEMBER

GOD, LOADED WITH GIFTS

SOMEONE wrote that God is loaded with gifts to give to people, but there are very few takers. God has a special gift for each one of us, if only we will open our hearts to receive it. For you it might be peace of mind, guidance, comfort, forgiveness, joy, as your personal gift.

In this season of giving and receiving of gifts, will you receive what you need from the generous overloaded arms of God? You will gladden his heart as well as enriching your own life.

Then there is your special gift of service to others as a member of the Church, the body of Christ (see Romans 12:7, Ephesians 4:12). It is an exciting experience to find that we can be used of God in some special way.

Ask for God's guidance in this matter.

Along the Way

7 DECEMBER

WINNING OTHERS

MASTER, I should like to have a long talk with You
    about this subject,
for You know best all that is involved.
Many of us long to win souls for You.
From the standpoint of youth it seemed
a challenging and concrete cause –
getting others to accept You
    as Saviour and Lord.

Master, how do You regard Your mission on earth?
You loved with supreme love,
    You died to save us
yet You were betrayed, deserted and crucified.
The net result of Your arduous campaigning
    for the Kingdom of God
was a handful of muscular fishermen
    and some devoted women,
but from that unpromising beginning
    sprang the Christian Church.

Are we too hurried, too impatient
in wanting to get results for our labours?
To see the corn ripening in the fields
    we have only just sown?
To count the sheaves and enter the statistics?

Teach us, Master, that winning others is slow work
      and each small step is vital.
A handshake, a smile, a word, a prayer,
      a text from Your Book,
strengthening this one's faith, sharing some sorrow,
building up the Kingdom brick by brick,
not erecting a pre-fab ordered complete,
but working slowly for eternal gains.

God in My Everyday

8 DECEMBER

A WAY OF ESCAPE

CHORE after chore until I am weary . . .
Is that all that life holds, Master?
A long line of tasks stretching out
      into the known future and much further . . .
         into the space of the unknown rest of my days.
However, You remind me that there are ways of escape
      without neglecting duty.

Memory is a way of escape while hands are busy
      with monotonous movements.
Thoughts can flash to happy scenes in the past.
Planning for the future can be a way of escape.
      Glowing dreams of what might be
speed away the hours and quotas are achieved.

Praying is a way of escape, making a tedious job
      into an offering to You, Lord.
You, who on earth toiled at a carpenter's bench
      with familiar tools
      held in competent hands.
You were preparing Yourself
      for Your redemptive mission,
      while the sawdust drifted down
to coat the floor in fragrant softness.

At least I can lift my heart to You and ask
      for courage to continue,
      for faith to hold fast,
      for peace of mind . . .
and that will be a way of escape from dull monotony
into a joyous moment of contact with You.

God in My Everyday

A GOOD PROGRAMME

I HAD switched off, not knowing it was coming;
>
> so I lost a treat, something that would have brought me
>> joy,
>
> moments wonderful to experience
> and enriching to remember; but

I had switched off.

> That happens, too, Lord, when You speak to me.
> I don't always hear
> because I don't always listen.

I have switched off my spiritual receiver.

And times of enrichment pass me by
>
> leaving me unmoved, unchanged.
> I have no one to blame, the fault is my own.
> I wasn't receptive to You just then,
> and my life is impoverished, just that bit poorer,
> because I wasn't listening.

I had switched off.

Help me to keep my heart open to You, Lord,
>
> my spirit receptive,
> my soul at its listening post.
> For You have much to say to me,
> things that I need to know,
> words for my strengthening, guidance for my way.

Keep me tuned in, Master, listening, waiting,
>
> eager to receive;
> and ready to act on
> all that You have to say to me.

Just a Moment, Lord

SNOW

MASTER, Your creation reveals some exquisite designs,
>
> but none more elaborate than the snowflakes
> in their crystalline beauty,
>
each one different in billions of variations.
>
> How snow changes the landscape!
>
It softens contours, beautifies ugliness
and clothes even a broken branch with grace.

Thank you, Lord, for such panoramas of
          pure white loveliness.
Of course, when we are struggling along against a blizzard
we are not conscious of the delicate tracery
          of the individual snowflake,
such as the microscope reveals.
Snow *en masse* is an obstacle,
          in drifts it is a menace, too much creates disaster.

I sometimes wonder, Lord, if you look
          with a certain lack of interest
          at a hodgepodge of humanity
pouring out of a commuter train or factory,
massed in a football stadium or crowding summer beaches.
Are we simply a *conglomeration* to you,
          a horde with a composite identity?
Or are we still individuals known personally
          to you?
With the snowflake in mind, Lord, I dare to believe
that as you have made us each unique,
we are never lost from you in a crowd,
never bunched together so tightly that we lose
          our individuality.
These are random thoughts, Master, as the snowflakes
          drift past my window.
But somehow they are comforting.

My God and I

UNIQUE

ON arrival in Chile in 1949, we had to register with the police. Our photograph was taken – with a number plate across the chest. Fingers and thumbs were blackened with ink and we had to make impressions on half a dozen forms. To get the ink off our fingers was a long and arduous job. But there, on those papers we were identified beyond any possibility of doubt.

You are different from everyone else. You are unique! A creation of God in a new mould and from a new pattern. Does not that give you special worth? You are a new combination of many possibilities, a new link in the chain of life, unlike any that have gone before.

Lift up your head then, straighten your back. Look life in the face and determine to make the best of it.

Hints for Living

RETIREMENT

IT'S happened! I'm retired, Lord.
A senior citizen with all the rights and privileges
      of that august and growing group.
Leisure unending for the rest of my days!
No need to get up in the chill of dawn when the alarm rings,
      to go out in pelting rain to catch a bus,
or miss a good T.V. programme because of duties . . .
      Hooray for freedom!

But You know, Lord, that I'm an energetic person,
      I just can't be idle.
My hands or my brain must work or I'm unhappy
      so I need Your help to plan my days,
to choose what I shall do
      to fill my time pleasurably and profitably.
Age is of course a great help in this
      for I do everything more slowly than before.

You know how I used to rush about, Master,
doing three things at once while I planned more.
It's funny how long it takes me to do *one* thing now
      and that makes time pass.
If visitors are coming for lunch I have to start
      to prepare the day before;
I, who used to whisk together a meal in half an hour.

Slowly and surely has to be my motto today.
There must be time to pause, to think, to pray . . .
How lovely to have time to commune with You
      without watching the clock!
To have time to re-read old books that have meant so much
and to nod with deepened understanding
      at the marginal notes made in youth.
Thank You, Lord, for this gracious sunset of life.
Help me to use it wisely.

Between You and Me, Lord

HEALTH FOODS

HEALTH foods are so easy and even . . . Excuse me a moment but I must
just rinse my mung bean sprouts growing lustily in the airing cupboard. As

I was saying, health foods are . . . oh dear! I've forgotten to start off the yoghurt and I need it for breakfast tomorrow. Health foods are so easy to provide in the home, because . . . no, surely not! I've omitted to water the mustard and cress on the kitchen window sill. I must dash off to see if I can rescue it from dry death . . . It was wilting but not too far gone to save. I was remarking that health foods are easy once you . . . There! If I haven't forgotten to mix up a new supply of breakfast muesli of my special home-made brand. I emptied the jar this morning.

Phew! I'm worn out with keeping myself healthy!

Along the Way

COMPOST COMFORT

LORD, I've had my hands deep into compost,
hands duly covered by rubber gloves, of course.
It was a most satisfying experience
    awaking thoughts of You.

As I worked to get the rich dark soil
    distributed over the garden,
    slow delight filled my soul.
I was down to life's basics,
    touching the eternal order of things,
nature's recycling into new beginnings.
As I toiled I worshipped,
keenly aware of Your purpose in the world,
to take the spent, the withered, the dead
    and to transform it into something vital and life-giving.

That is destiny for the human part of me, I know, Lord;
    'ashes to ashes, dust to dust . . . '
those words seem very chilly and unfeeling today.
This warm brown loam between my fingers gives them the lie
for it bears rich nourishment for future plants and flowers,
    food for birds, animals and man.

On that dull December day,
    my gardening gloves still earthy,
I came into the house with glowing joy in my heart,
    a wordless rapture which endured
    long after my muddy boots had been put away.
Thank You, Lord, for that moment of communion,
    the comforting message of the compost heap.

Between You and Me, Lord

225

PEACE

HOW could you, Lord, speak of inward peace
when the snares of wicked men were closing round You
and a stark cross loomed ahead?

From what hidden spring did You drink?
What inward resources gave You Your strength?
    I'd like to know Your secret, Lord,
      for I, too, need Your peace.

Not the stillness of a graveyard, a dead peace;
not cloistered serenity, the peace of withdrawal;
not the calm that narcotics give, a doped peace;
it's Your peace I want, Master.

The peace of a clear conscience,
    of a disciplined life,
      an integrated character.
The peace of vigorous action in a righteous cause,
    a vibrant, joyous peace.
You spoke of peace as a gift, Lord.
Can anyone receive it from You?
Can I? In spite of my frustrations,
    in spite of my anxieties,
    in spite of my failures?

Dare I ask You for it? Just now, Lord?
Yes, just now.

Just a Moment, Lord

BLESSING THE LORD

THE Psalmist exhorts us to bless the Lord at all times. We so often pray, 'O Lord, bless the needy, the sick, refugees and orphan children . . . ' that the word 'bless' seems to cover a lot of different meanings.

I have often wondered how we humans can 'bless' the Lord.

The Psalmist helps us in our thinking by continuing: 'His praise shall continually be in my mouth.' So 'blessing the Lord' means praising him for his grace and mercy. To that I would add: thanking him for his forgiving love. Further, it could include a fresh yielding of ourselves to him, a renewed forging of a link of communion by a quietening of the soul in prayer.

What a lot of meanings the word 'bless' contains!

Along the Way

THE TIME FACTOR

WHEN facing an unpleasant or boring job – and which of us doesn't have to do that? – I have found it helpful to set myself a reasonable time limit in which to complete it, and then to work against that dead-line and try to beat it.

It is a harmless game to play with oneself, but it helps when tackling a mundane job that has to be done.

Along the Way

DEATH BUT A DOOR

MASTER, I thank You,
for You have removed a black cloud from my horizon
    by taking from me the fear of death.
I have come to realise that death is but a door,
a door into the larger, fuller life of the spirit.
Through that door we all have to pass.
    One day it will be my turn but I am not afraid.

What awaits me on the other side?
    I wish I knew more . . .
It is a strange thought that I shall embark on that last journey
    with no ticket, no luggage and no money,
I who have always made such careful preparations
    for every little trip.
This time there will be just me . . . and You.

I can never think of Heaven as 'up there'
    for it's around us now,
    in another dimension closed to our earthly senses.
In escaping from the body we qualify to enter
    the realm of the spirit.
It will be a fantastic adventure,
    like a baby thrust from the womb to the world.

Don't let my loved ones sorrow for me when I go, Lord.
Let them think of me emerging into more abundant life
    with much greater fulfilment
    and added joys.
Let them remember that I shall still be in Your hands,
    still the object of Your love and care,
    and let their hearts be comforted.

Between You and Me, Lord

AFTER THE STORM

YESTERDAY, Lord, it stormed all day!
    Dark skies, slashing rain,
    fierce winds and floods.
The world of nature seemed in chaos
    and my heart trembled.

Today is quite different, Master.
The sun shines, the skies are clear
and chubby white clouds drift dreamily
across the pale blue heavens.
    How my heart rejoices!

Storms come . . . and storms pass.
That is the lesson I must learn afresh.
It is good that I am reminded of it
    for life has other storms . . .
sudden crises, accidents and disasters,
    disillusions and disappointments.
These crush my heart with fear as they pound out
    their message of doom.
Yet they too will pass
    and possibly be forgotten.

Calm my heart, Lord, in the midst of the storm.
Say to me: 'Why are you afraid? Trust Me,
    I will help you through.'
Thank You, Master, for that word.

God in My Everyday

THE REAL ME

WHICH is the real me, Master?
I ought to know myself for we have been linked
    for many years
but suddenly an accidental happening,
    some disappointment
    or unexpected news,
shows me to myself in another light
and I am glad – sometimes –
or appalled – most of the time –
    at what I find within.

Which is the real me, Lord?
Is there any 'real me' at all?
Am I like an onion covered
        in layer after layer,
           growing smaller and smaller
until the heart is reached?

You know me, Lord, right through
        all my protective skins.
I shudder when I think of all You know,
those things I can hide from others
who only see the outward stance.
In moments of intimate talk
        friends may glimpse another me,
but only Your eyes pierce to the centre.
What do You find there?

Only You can bring integration, Master,
welding my being into wholeness,
an all-through genuineness of thought,
        act and will.
Do it for me, Lord!

God in My Everyday

21 December

UNI-BUTTONING

ISN'T it about time we adopted Uni-buttoning for our clothes? Is it reasonable, in these days, to perpetuate the old fashioned buttoning on different sides for men and women? The zip is sexless and acceptable to all. Why not a common buttoning policy? Gone are the days when men had to use their left hand to button their doublets, or whatever else they wore, leaving the right hand grasping the hilt of a sword to defend fair ladies from attack.

This became a problem for me recently when I bought uniform shirts for my two Danish grandchildren, each buttoning a different way according to sex. Ridiculous! What clothing manufacturer will inaugurate unisex buttoning, and when can we expect it?

But stay! Shall we ladies give in to the men and button the left side over, or will the men cede the point to us ladies? Who will be willing to change? Perhaps the difficulty of resolving that question reveals why the matter has not been dealt with earlier.

Along the Way

ONE DAY A WEEK

I HAVE made a new resolve. On one day a week I will look at the flowers in my garden and not at the weeds; I'll stop to admire a single rose instead of noting the greenfly or the black spot on the leaves and I will look at my pictures and ornaments, instead of the dust on them.

And why this sudden burst of good resolution? I discovered that I was concentrating on what was wrong instead of on what was right. I decided to mend my ways – at least one day a week for a start!

Along the Way

ENJOYMENT

TODAY, Master, I will enjoy Your world.
Many times I wander through the hours
      busy with this and that
but not absorbing my surroundings.
Today is going to be different!
Today I pledge myself to enjoy
      colour and tone
      sound and smell
      light and shade
      taste and touch
      shape and texture.
What a lot of good things this old world holds!

Deepen my awareness, Lord!
Let me respond more readily to my environment.
Let me see with new appreciation,
hear with more intent listening,
taste, savouring with my tongue,
feel with sensitised fingers
      the angular, the curved,
      the rough, the smooth.

Why! even one room can become
      an exciting place to explore
if I use all my sharpened senses.

I will rest in Your joyous presence, Lord.
Safe in the shelter of Your love
      I will enjoy Your world
with all its delights and surprises.

God in My Everyday

SLOW DAWNING

IN my daily Bible reading I like to underline words that have special meaning for me or a relevant message to my own heart.

I found marked in Titus 2:11 (*NEB*) the glorious phrase: 'For the grace of God has dawned upon the world with healing for all mankind.' And in Titus 3:4 the same theme of dawning reappears: 'the kindness and generosity of God our Saviour dawned upon the world'. To me this spoke of God's revelation of himself to mankind, as people were able to receive it; a slow dawning of wondrous beauty and power.

How often we say, 'Today it *dawned* upon me that . . . '! How obtuse we are, how reluctant and sluggish to accept God's dawning revelation!

In these days of giving, let us think of the *generosity* of God who gave his own Son to be incarnate in our world.

Along the Way

WHAT'S THE DATE? (CHRISTMAS)

YOU made quite a local impact, Master,
when as a babe You joined the human race in Bethlehem.
Wondrous tales abound of stars, angels,
        shepherds and wise men
all accompanying Your advent.

Many people do not believe that story.
They scoff at the Christmas gospel while enjoying
        Christmas festivities.
But while they scoff, they acknowledge You,
        You who they say never existed.
Every time they say: 'What's the date?'
        they are asking: 'When was Jesus born?'
Each time they date a letter, they pay silent homage
        to Your coming.
Before Christ and After Christ . . . so is history divided.
BC and AD – Anno Domini – Year of our Lord.

Master, I pray at this festive season that someone
        who has lived quite factually
        'before Christ' in their lives
will take the personal decisive step into AD,
        Year of our Lord,
acknowledging You as Saviour and King.

God in My Everyday

LEISURE

LEISURE is frightening, Master:
    a string of empty hours,
    a missing day in the almanac,
    a blank page in life's book.
The stream of time slipping unnoticed through careless fingers;
    nothing thought,
    nothing experienced,
    nothing achieved.

A long road leading nowhere, sprouting useless cul-de-sacs;
    no direction,
    no purpose,
    no goal.

Help me to use leisure wisely, Lord,
    to enjoy Your beautiful world,
    to learn more of Your marvellous creation;
    to enrich my mind,
    to water friendship's garden.

For one day I shall have to give account
    to none other than to You, Lord,
    how I have used the gift of time.
    Time to work, to rest, to play,
    time to serve others and enjoy others.

You will ask me not only what I have done,
    but what I have left undone.

Help me then not to waste one single moment.
    And when no taskmaster stands over me,
    when I am left to my own devices,
    let me use leisure wisely,
    knowing for that too
    You will hold me to account.

Just a Moment, Lord

27 December

GOOD CHEER

ONE gloomy, rainy morning I waited for a bus with another obvious pensioner. When it came it overshot the stopping place so we had to run for a few steps to board it. The cheery, booming voice of the conductor challenged us two oldies: 'Come along, you youngsters, put a spurt on! If you can't do better than that now, how will it be when you are old?'

There were broad smiles on all faces in the bus, including our own, as this happy conductor jollied us along. When my companion showed her travel permit he held it up at arm's length, then said as he returned it: 'It doesn't do you credit, madam. You're much better looking!'

It was a refreshing start to a wintry day to meet so much good humour emanating from a single individual and spreading to all around.

I almost wished my journey had been longer than four stops!

Along the Way

MIST ON THE HILS

MIST on the hills!
Fog on the roads,
the outlook gloomy with a sense of unreality.
An uncomfortable feeling of being choked,
enclosed by a stifling grey blanket.

Teach me to live on my memories, Lord.
To picture the distant mountain,
the sunlight glinting on the river,
patterned by the wake of small boats.

The unseen is there, is real and living!
Let me rejoice in that knowledge and await;
clarity of vision will return.

So, too, Lord, let it be in my spiritual life.
When clouds imprison me
and faith is dulled;
when love is cold
and truth seems dead.

Then let me call to mind Your former graciousness;
moments when my heart responded,
when my soul rejoiced in Your presence,
my faith shone bright and firm.

The unseen is there, is real and living!
Let me rejoice in that knowledge and await;
clarity of vision will return.

Just a Moment, Lord

29 DECEMBER

FOOTSTEPS IN THE SNOW

ON a delightful morning, with newly fallen snow on the ground and the sun shining from a pale blue sky, I made my way across a park to do my shopping. When I returned a little later, there were my footprints plainly visible across the snowy grass.

But what a surprise I got!

I would have been prepared to swear in a law court that I had walked straight across the grass, but the footprints showed a very wobbly line. I saw I had deviated several times from the straight beeline I thought I was making. I shall have to do better in facing this new year to 'run the straight race through God's good grace'.

I wish you a good beginning to the new year and a sense of God's presence every day.

Along the Way

30 DECEMBER

TOMORROW

TOMORROW is an x-day, Lord,
an unknown quantity of unknown quality.
I'm not even sure that there will be a tomorrow.
        It's a might-be, not a shall-be.
So far in my life sunrise has always followed sunset,
        but it won't always be so.

What does tomorrow conceal in its travelling bag?
        Joyous surprises?
        Let them all come.
        Good news?
        I'm thirsting for it.

Or there might possibly be sorrows . . .
        the death of a loved one?
If so, help me to be grateful for the hours we shared,
let memories bind a golden chain.
        Is sickness in the offing?
Let me learn lessons of patience and endurance.

Catastrophe may suddenly strike me:
        road accident?
        train wreck?
        air disaster?
        who knows?

Life has many ingredients, some good, some bad.
All kinds must come my way at some time.

Keep my heart steady, Lord, whatever tomorrow may
        bring.
Let me hold Your hand and walk unafraid with You;
for finally, Master, You will write one word
      over my earthly life,
      and that word will be
      FINIS.

Just a Moment, Lord

31 DECEMBER

A NEW DIARY (YEAR'S END)

WHAT have I written, Lord, in my diary
      for the past twelve months?
Dare I open the book to see?
As I turn the pages I find with surprise
      that many are blank!
Days when I did nothing except . . .
      pass the hours
      in monotonous routine.
Nothing outstanding in thought or deed,
      nothing worth recording.

Other pages are badly blotted.
I was trying to achieve some goal,
      perhaps set by others
      or of my own choosing.
I tried and failed . . . and tried again,
      then gave up in disgust.
A few of the pages are heavily altered
      with many deletions.
Strong reactions to persons or circumstances,
      hot, rebellious days
when I scythed my way through opposition.

The year is at an end and the book is finished.
Not one entry can I now change, Master.
Tomorrow I open a new diary, its pages
      invitingly clean.
I stiffen my will with firm determination.
Help me, Lord, to live the new year worthily.

God in My Everyday

Works by Flora Larsson

Prayer poems

Just a Moment, Lord	1973	(Hodder and Stoughton)
Between You and Me, Lord	1975	(Hodder and Stoughton)
Towards You, Lord	1978	(Hodder and Stoughton)
God in My Everyday	1984	(Hodder and Stoughton)
My God and I	1993	(SP&S Ltd)

Books published by SP&S Ltd:

Short biographies

Always Ready to Sail (Alfred Benwell)	1958
Viking Warrior (Karl Larsson)	1959
Queen of the Barge (Georgette Gogibus)	1960
God's Man in Devil's Island (Charles Péan)	1960
Ruth goes to the Congo (Ruth Siegfried)	1961

Other works

My Best Men are Women	1974
From My Treasure Chest	1981

Index of Titles

Title	*Book or Series*	*Date*
Art	Along the Way	5 Jul
Autumn ecstasy	Between You and Me	14 Oct
Bargaining	My God and I	3 Sep
Becoming rich	God in My Everyday	20 Oct
Begin again (New Year)	God in My Everyday	1 Jan
Bereft	Towards You, Lord	26-30 Sep
Between you and me	Between You and Me	27 Apr
Big me	Just a Moment, Lord	2 May
Blessing the Lord	Along the Way	16 Dec
Bondage	God in My Everyday	29 Oct
Book friends	Between You and Me	11 Jan
Born good	Towards You, Lord	1 Jul
Boxes	Between You and Me	14 Jul
Braggart	Just a Moment, Lord	6 May
Bringing up Grandma	Along the Way	15 Sep
Buttons	Between You and Me	14 Aug
Changing moods	Hints for Living	25 Apr
Clutter	My God and I	27 Aug
Coals of fire	Towards You, Lord	11 Jun
Coils of sin	Down Memory Lane	22 Mar
Colour	Between You and Me	8 Jun
Commitment	My God and I	5 Jun
Compensations	Along the Way	16 Jun
Compost comfort	Between You and Me	14 Dec
Conquest	Along the Way	8 Feb
Controlled	Hints for Living	2 Jul
Cooking for one	Between You and Me	16 Aug
Courage	Down Memory Lane	19 May
Courage for today	Towards You, Lord	4 Aug
Courage to live	Just a Moment, Lord	30 Jan
Credit cards	God in My Everyday	24 Jun
Criticism	Towards You, Lord	2 Aug
Crutches	My God and I	4 Oct
Curtains	Between You and Me	22 Sep
Danger ahead	Along the Way	23 May
Dangling leaves	Between You and Me	1 Dec
Dark glasses	God in My Everyday	12 Jun
Death but a door	Between You and Me	18 Dec
Demolition	Between You and Me	4 Dec
Develop yourself	Hints for Living	27 Mar
Distorted vision	Down Memory Lane	4 Apr
Divine patience	My God and I	28 Aug
Divorce	My God and I	18 Nov
Do you listen?	Just a Moment, Lord	20 Jan
Doing without	Along the Way	9 Nov
Don't wear a halo	Along the Way	13 Feb
Doorstep surprise	Along the Way	8 Sep
Double glazing	My God and I	6 Oct

239

Title	Book or Series	Date
Praying away locusts	Down Memory Lane	24 Apr
Preview of spring	Along the Way	11 Nov
Price tab	God in My Everyday	13 Sep
Prick of conscience	My God and I	6 Aug
Problems	Along the Way	2 Dec
Progress	Towards You, Lord	4 Mar
Quick results	Towards You, Lord	21 Nov
Quickie prayers	Along the Way	16 May
Rapture	Between You and Me	10 Nov
Regrets	Between You and Me	7 Jan
Rejection	Towards You, Lord	11 Aug
Relax a bit	Hints for Living	29 Apr
Relaxation (1)	My God and I	28 Jun
Relaxation (2)	Hints for Living	30 Jun
Relaxation (3)	Hints for Living	8 Jul
Relief	Between You and Me	9 Mar
Retirement	Between You and Me	12 Dec
Right as rain	Along the Way	11 Oct
Runaway horses	Down Memory Lane	9 Apr
Saint in embryo	Just a Moment, Lord	1 May
Saints	Towards You, Lord	[29 Feb]
Save £££s	Along the Way	28 Jan
Self-acceptance	Towards You, Lord	21 May
Self-discipline	Hints for Living	23 Jun
Self-pity	Just a Moment, Lord	3 May
Shortages	From My Treasure Chest	23 Feb
Sickness	Hints for Living	13 May
Sidetracks	Just a Moment, Lord	18 Jan
Silence	God in My Everyday	26 Jun
Silent heroism	God in My Everyday	24 May
Sitting lightly to life	Between You and Me	8 Nov
Slander	My God and I	24 Oct
Slow dawning	Along the Way	24 Dec
Snow	My God and I	10 Dec
Snowdrops	My God and I	1 Feb
Someone to listen	Just a Moment, Lord	26 Jan
Someone's pet corn	Just a Moment, Lord	22 Apr
Soul and body	God in My Everyday	14 Apr
Spaces	Along the Way	29 Jul
Spare parts	God in My Everyday	27 Jul
Spectacles	My God and I	2 Oct
Spiritual pigmy	Hints for Living	27 Jun
Spiritual vitamins	Along the Way	26 Jul
Spring cleaning	Between You and Me	24 Mar
Stabs of remembrance	Towards You, Lord	28 Sep
Stand up and be counted	Down Memory Lane	15 Feb
Stay-at-homes	Along the Way	15 Jul
Step by step	Between You and Me	11 May